INTO THE DEEP

SCIENCE, TECHNOLOGY, AND THE QUEST TO PROTECT THE OCEAN

CHRISTY PETERSON

TWENTY-FIRST CENTURY BOOKS / MINNEAPOLIS

For Ruth. Thank you for your friendship and your passion for the ocean.

Twenty-First Century Books™
An imprint of Lerner Publishing Group, Inc.
241 First Avenue North
Minneapolis, MN 55401 USA
For reading levels and more information, look up this title at www.lernerbooks.com.

Main body text set in News Gothic Com Roman.
Typeface provided by Linotype AG.

Library of Congress Cataloging-in-Publication Data

Names: Peterson, Christy, author. | Twenty-First Century Books (Firm)
Title: Into the deep : science, technology, and the quest to protect the ocean / Christy Peterson.
Description: Minneapolis : Twenty-First Century Books, [2020] | Includes bibliographical references and index. | Audience: Ages: 13–18. | Audience: Grades: 9 to 12.
Identifiers: LCCN 2019020685 (print) | LCCN 2019981277 (ebook) | ISBN 9781541555556 (library binding : alk. paper) | ISBN 9781541583849 (ebook)
Subjects: LCSH: Ocean. | Oceanography. | Marine ecology. | Marine biology. | Marine resources—Management. | Restoration ecology. | Underwater exploration. | Climate change mitigation.
Classification: LCC GC21 .P29 2020 (print) | LCC GC21 (ebook) | DDC 551.46—dc23

LC record available at https://lccn.loc.gov/2019020685
LC ebook record available at https://lccn.loc.gov/2019981277

Manufactured in the United States of America
1-46010-42927-10/1/2019

CONTENTS

ACKNOWLEDGMENTS

I want to thank the generous scientists, researchers, and technicians who made this book possible by patiently explaining their work and answering the endless questions of an enthusiastic layperson. Without them, this book would not have been possible. Any mistakes are my own.

Megan Scanderbeg, Scripps Institution of
    Oceanography, California

Emery Nolasco, Monterey Bay Aquarium Research
    Institute, California

Jennifer B. Paduan, Monterey Bay Aquarium Research
    Institute, California

Dr. Eleanor Frajka-Williams, National Oceanography Centre, UK

Jonathan Peter Fram, Oregon State University, Oregon

Dr. Jack Barth, Oregon State University, Oregon

Flora Vincent, PhD, Weizmann Institute of Science, Israel

Dr. Petra H. Lenz, University of Hawaiʻi at Mānoa, Hawaiʻi

Dr. Vittoria Roncalli, University of Barcelona, Spain

Dr. Eva Majerová, University of Hawai'i, Hawai'i

Larry Hufnagle, NOAA NWFSC, Washington

Dr. Kim Martini, Sea-Bird Scientific, Washington

Dr. Tracey Sutton, Nova Southeastern University, Florida

Nina Pruzinsky, Nova Southeastern University, Florida

Dr. Rupert Collins, University of Bristol, UK

Dr. Leigh Torres, Oregon State University, Oregon

Dr. Maureen H. Conte, Marine Biological
      Laboratory, Massachusetts

Dr. Rut Pedrosa Pàmies, Marine Biological
      Laboratory, Massachusetts

J. C. Weber, Marine Biological Laboratory, Massachusetts

Dr. Andrew Shao, University of Victoria, Canada

Additional thanks to Ruth Musgrave, Robert Tuck, and my
family—I couldn't have done it without you.

INTRODUCTION

On January 21, 2018, a woman walking along a sandy beach in Western Australia noticed a dark brown bottle partially buried in the sand. Thinking it might make a unique decoration for her home, she retrieved it and showed it to her family. The discovery proved to be more intriguing than expected. Inside the bottle, covered in damp sand, lay a tightly wrapped roll of paper secured with twine.

The family feared that unwrapping the damp paper might damage the document, so they dried it in the oven. Then they carefully unrolled it to reveal the contents: a combination of typeset and handwritten text. Written in German, the preprinted portion included instructions to ship the bottle back to the German Naval Observatory in Hamburg. The handwritten section recorded the ship's name, the *Paula*; the ship's home port, Elsfleth; its port of departure, Cardiff; and its destination, Makassar. It also noted the location where the bottle went overboard. But the most surprising portion of the message was the date—June 12, 1886.

Was the bottle a fantastic piece of history or just an elaborate hoax? The family turned to the Western Australian Museum for assistance. The museum discovered that the bottle—a gin bottle made in the Netherlands—did indeed date from the late nineteenth century. And experts in Germany confirmed that a ship named *Paula* set sail from Cardiff bound for Makassar in 1886. They located the ship's meteorological journal, which contained an entry for June 12, 1886, noting the deployment of a drift bottle. The handwriting in the journal exactly matched the paper found in the bottle.

The experts determined that the bottle had been part of an experiment conceived by German scientist Georg von Neumayer, who wanted to know more about ocean currents. He hoped this research would help shipping companies move goods around the world more efficiently. Beginning in 1864, commercial ships deployed more than 6,000 bottles. Of those, 662 eventually found their way back to Germany. The 663rd bottle, found in 2018, is on loan to the Western Australia Museum.

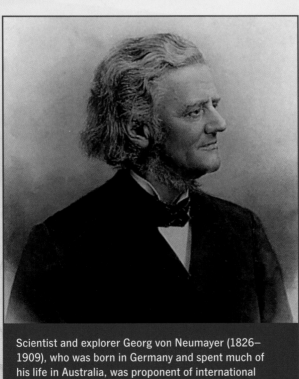

Scientist and explorer Georg von Neumayer (1826–1909), who was born in Germany and spent much of his life in Australia, was proponent of international collaboration and cooperation in scientific endeavors.

TECH FOCUS:
NOAA DRIFTERS AND ARGO FLOATS

Scientists continue to use drift bottle studies, but they have significant limitations. Only a small percentage of the bottles find their way back to researchers. They also only record two data points: where they started and where they ended up. Because most bottles float, winds influence their movement much more than surface currents do. In the middle of the twentieth century, scientists began developing more sophisticated "bottles" that could be reliably tracked and record far more data. They resulted in two new kinds of tools that expand upon Georg von Neumayer's efforts.

Drifting buoys, or drifters, bob along like a glass bottle, but that is where the similarity ends. A drifter has a long, cylinder-shaped tail. This allows the buoy to move with ocean currents below rather than with the winds above. The drifter includes scientific instruments that record location as well as barometric pressure, temperature, salinity, and other details about the water's chemistry. Data are uploaded to satellites.

One project that uses drifter technology is the Global Drifter Program operated by National Oceanic and Atmospheric Administration (NOAA). On May 1, 2018, the program deployed its twenty-five hundredth drifter. The information collected by NOAA drifters gives a real-time overview of ocean conditions, helps improve weather forecasts, and offers scientists a way to verify the accuracy of measurements made by other instruments, such as satellites.

The second type of updated "bottle" allows scientists to collect data from much deeper in the water column, a given vertical expanse of water between the surface and the seafloor. Neutrally buoyant floats sink to a certain depth and hold their position for a time specified in their programming. Then, as they rise to the surface, they gather information about water temperature and chemistry. At the surface, the floats relay data they've gathered to a satellite.

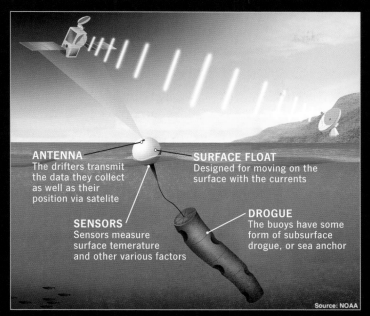

ANTENNA
The drifters transmit the data they collect as well as their position via satelite

SURFACE FLOAT
Designed for moving on the surface with the currents

SENSORS
Sensors measure surface temerature and other various factors

DROGUE
The buoys have some form of subsurface drogue, or sea anchor

Source: NOAA

This illustration of an ocean drifter shows where each of the components involved in taking and transmitting measurements are located.

Argo, a worldwide project named for a ship in Greek mythology, uses a fleet of floats to gather data about subsurface currents and conditions. Argo floats measure temperature, pressure, and salinity. A new float design that recently joined the fleet also carries sensors that measure other factors including pH, oxygen, and chlorophyll. Scientists deployed the first Argo float in 2000. By January 2019, nearly four thousand floats launched by institutions from countries around the world spread out over the ocean. Scientists are using the data collected over the last twenty years to track ocean changes. The longer the period, the more confident scientists can be in their results.

View the status of the Argo array with Google Earth by following the instructions on Argo's website, http://www.Argo.ucsd.edu/Argo_GE.html.

Von Neumayer was not the first to throw bottles overboard to study ocean currents. The earliest known drift bottle study occurred in 310 BCE when Greek philosopher Theophrastus tossed sealed bottles overboard to prove that water flowing in from the Atlantic Ocean had formed the Mediterranean Sea. However, the German study coincided with the earliest days of a new area of science: oceanography. The bottle unearthed on an Australian beach 132 years after it was tossed overboard was part of an early attempt to understand the ocean in a new way.

UNDERSTANDING THE OCEAN—PAST AND PRESENT

Humans have been intimately tied to the ocean for thousands of years. Coastal communities learned to time their activities to get the best catches of fish and shellfish. They learned to harvest salt from the ocean for seasoning and food preservation. And they used seaweed and other marine materials to craft objects like fishing lines and jewelry, as well as for food and fertilizer.

Humans also used the ocean as transport. Fish bones and tools uncovered on islands in the Mediterranean and in Indonesia suggest that humans and their ancient cousins, Neanderthals and *Homo erectus*, may have traveled by water at least 130,000 years ago. Ancient Polynesian people, considered expert ancient mariners, mastered the art of reading ocean currents and using the positions of stars and the sun to navigate across vast distances. Originating in the islands of the eastern Pacific, they colonized the islands of Micronesia and Melanesia about 3,500 years ago. By 400 CE they reached the Hawaiian Islands to the north and Easter Island to the east. They added New Zealand and the Chatham Islands to their vast community by 1000 CE, effectively populating 800,000 square miles (2 million sq. km) of the Pacific Ocean almost 400 years before Europe's major age of ocean exploration began.

Evidence left by ancient mariners, along with stories passed through the generations, demonstrates that humans learned enough about the ocean to derive their livelihoods from its waters and to travel widely. But the formal study of oceanography that emerged in the late nineteenth century seeks to understand the ocean in the modern, scientific sense—to analyze and quantify its movements, composition, and influence on the planet and to understand the life that calls it home.

Von Neumayer's six thousand drifting bottles were part of this new approach to ocean exploration. Over the last century, teams of scientists, researchers, and technology experts have developed increasingly sophisticated and sensitive tools and have deployed them across the entire globe, from satellites peering down from space to drills boring through the seabed. These tools help us understand the physical ocean, from how much water the ocean holds to the chemical makeup of water and its movement around the globe to the organisms that live in the ocean, from microscopic viruses and bacteria to some of the largest creatures that ever lived on Earth.

Scientists and their tools have helped us understand how profoundly the ocean impacts the planet. Thanks to their work, we know that the ocean feeds the water cycle, moves heat energy from the equator toward the poles, drives weather patterns, feeds and employs millions of people, and supplies about 50 percent of the oxygen we breathe.

A RACE TO UNDERSTAND AND PROTECT

But just as we're learning how the ocean affects us and every other living thing on the planet, no matter how far inland, we are also seeing that the ocean faces threats from all sides. Agricultural runoff entering the ocean from rivers and streams creates vast "dead zones" where little life exists. Rising ocean temperatures threaten sea life and alter currents. Melting ice caps raise the sea level, which may displace millions of people worldwide. Plastic waste entering all levels of the food web is killing organisms from plankton to whales and

A WORD ABOUT CLIMATE CHANGE

Scientists began to sound the alarm about climate change about forty years ago, but the idea that humans were causing unprecedented changes to the Earth's atmosphere appeared much earlier. In 1896 scientist Svante Arrhenius speculated that burning fossil fuels could raise temperatures worldwide. Scientists recognized in the 1950s that burning fossil fuels was leading to increased atmospheric CO_2. By the mid-1960s, military and oil industry–sponsored studies had already suggested that increased CO_2 levels due to fossil fuel combustion would lead to climate changes by the year 2000.

In the late 1970s, a group of scientists predicted that global temperatures would rise by 5.4°F (3°C) if nothing were done to curb the emission of CO_2 and other greenhouse gases. This prediction was updated by the UN Meteorological Organization in late 2018. According to the 2018 reports, the expected temperature rise is 5.4°F to 9.0°F (3°C to 5°C) by the end of the century.

Although many politicians and media personalities still question the reality of climate change and humanity's role in these changes, the overwhelming majority of scientists agree that climate change is human-caused and that Earth's inhabitants have been feeling its effects for some time. A 2016 study in the journal *Nature* showed that human activity began to warm the atmosphere between 1830 and 1850. Scientists have shifted their focus to understanding the exact roles the atmosphere, the ocean, the land, and the ice sheets play in the climate system. They are also examining how we can make the natural world and human communities more resilient in the face of rapidly changing climate conditions.

WHY IS THE OCEAN SO HARD TO EXPLORE?

Ocean exploration is a challenge for many reasons, but it comes down to three basic problems:

- The ocean is huge. If a ship wished to sail all 140 million square miles (363 million sq. km) of it, that ship would be at sea for hundreds of years.
- The ocean is dark. At about 3,280 feet (1,000 m), sunlight disappears entirely. The average depth of the ocean is about 12,080 feet (3,682 m).
- Ocean pressure limits access for human explorers. At its average depth, the pressure is about 370 times greater than what you would feel standing on the beach at sea level.

possibly harming humans. And the ocean has absorbed a significant percentage of the carbon dioxide (CO_2) humans have pumped into the atmosphere over the last century. This is changing the composition of the water itself.

To address these threats, we need more precise understanding of the ocean than ever before, but the ocean remains the least explored part of our planet. According the National Oceanic and Atmospheric Administration (NOAA), more than 80 percent of the ocean—over half the planet—remains "unmapped, unobserved, and unexplored." So there are huge holes in our knowledge in almost every area of oceanography. Our ignorance hampers our ability to understand fully how the ocean impacts the planet and us. It prevents us from knowing exactly how our activities are affecting the ocean and the life that calls it home. And it hinders our efforts to implement policies and practices that can protect the ocean and ultimately ourselves.

PROFILE: MEGAN SCANDERBEG

STAFF RESEARCH ASSOCIATE, SCRIPPS INSTITUTION OF OCEANOGRAPHY, CALIFORNIA

Megan Scanderbeg began her career as a high school physics teacher. Eventually her love of science brought her out of the classroom and to Scripps Institution of Oceanography, where she supports the Argo program.

As the scientific coordinator, Scanderbeg helps ensure the Argo Steering Team runs smoothly by maintaining their website, planning meetings, publishing newsletters and brochures, and more. As the cochair for the Data Management Team, she also helps to keep the data system functioning well. She says a typical day includes "writing material either for reports, instruction cookbooks, the website, emails, and outreach material. I also often have computer programs running that I need to check on or update. These do things like get Argo trajectory data, unpack it, quality control it, calculate the velocity, and put it into a usable format for others to look at."

Scanderbeg enjoys working "on an international project that can contribute so much to our understanding of the ocean." She hopes that her work and the project overall will "hopefully help people make good, informed decisions about how to treat the planet." She recommends that students interesting in pursuing any career in science contact "college or university professors that do research that seems interesting to them and ask to volunteer in their lab or group, or volunteer at a nearby aquarium or company. It helps to learn to write well and to code. Basically, I suggest . . . trying different jobs and volunteer experiences to find out what aspect of science they like doing the most. There are many roles besides just that of a professor that exist in science."

Scientists and engineers around the globe are working to fill the holes in our knowledge before it's too late. They hope their work will lead to better policies and regulations to protect the ocean from climate change, pollution, overfishing, and other human impacts. So scientists have unleashed a dizzying array of tools that glide, fly, float, crawl, magnify, count, analyze, and illuminate. This technology takes science farther into the deep than ever before. New data contributes to scientific discussion and government policies to protect our planet's defining feature—the ocean.

PART 1

THE PHYSICAL OCEAN

CHAPTER 1

ALL THE WATER IN THE WORLD

The ocean contains over 96 percent of Earth's approximately 353 quintillion gallons (1,336 quintillion L) of water. If you stand on the Pacific coast, where land and sea meet, it's not difficult to imagine this. The view to the west is water as far as you can see. Roaring waves crash into the shallows and fan out across the sand. Powerful winter storms barrel in from offshore, unleashing giant waves, torrential rain, and destructive wind. And water escapes the ocean in huge banks of fog and envelops beachside towns and forests.

Travel east, into the heart of the North American continent, and the ocean's influence seems to disappear. Land, not water, stretches as far as the eye can see. Wind gathers swirling twisters of dust. The loud buzz of cicadas replaces the roar of the surf. But even here, where vast prairies and winding rivers dominate the landscape, the ocean's influence can be felt. Water flowing in rivers, pulsing through sprinklers, and stored underground in aquifers has journeyed through the water cycle. It has all been in the ocean at one time.

According to the US Geological Survey, "The oceans supply about 90 percent of the evaporated water that goes into the water cycle." Water vapor in the atmosphere forms clouds, which move with air currents. Some of these clouds end up over land, dropping the water they contain as precipitation. Some water that falls to Earth finds its way rapidly to small streams, larger rivers, and then back to the ocean. Another portion of the water may take a more circuitous route, descending deep underground through porous rock to form reservoirs called aquifers, or taking a break in an ice sheet for a few thousand years. Eventually though, this water will also make its way back to the sea.

Life on Earth depends upon this cycle that transports water inland from the sea. As Earth's human population inches toward eight billion and the demand for water increases, knowing precisely where and how water is moving around the globe becomes increasingly important. Cities need to plan where to source drinking water and farmers need to know if irrigation water will be sufficient to raise crops.

Another concern is that melting ice is leading to rising sea levels worldwide, threatening coastal cities. Scientists, climate modelers, and government agencies need to know exactly where this water is coming from so they can estimate how fast and high the seas will rise, and plan accordingly. But until recently, measuring Earth's water supply was largely a boots-on-the-ground affair and not always precise. For example, changes in the Greenland

Scientists Andreas Muenchow (*left*) and Keith Nicholls (*right*) work on Petermann Glacier in Greenland on August 27, 2016. They installed data stations here a year ago to study how quickly the glacier's ice shelf is melting. Attached to the station is a cable that reaches from the surface of the glacier down to the bottom of the ocean. The cable has five sensors attached to it that measure temperature and salinity, which indicate melt rates.

and Antarctic ice sheets were observed by eye, but scientists struggled to assess the exact volume of ice or the amount lost due to melting. Although scientists have been able to precisely measure sea level since 1993, they had no way of knowing the specific source of rising water. On land, measurements primarily represented water supplies that could be reached and physically recorded. This left the status of deeper groundwater supplies largely a mystery.

Scientists needed a better way to track all water on Earth, and its movement around the planet, no matter where it is. Some help came from satellites, which could take detailed images of changes to oceans, ice sheets, lakes, and rivers from high in space.

RECYCLED RAIN

Evaporation from the ocean fuels most precipitation on Earth, but not always directly. A simple graphic of the water cycle often shows water evaporating over the ocean, clouds moving toward land, precipitation falling and making its way to streams and rivers, and water returning to the ocean via those streams and rivers.

Reality is, as usual, more complex. Water does travel from the ocean to land as clouds. These clouds deliver precipitation. However, this precipitation doesn't all end up in streams and rivers. Some of it evaporates, condenses again into clouds, and falls again as precipitation. This process can repeat many times before this water ends up back in the ocean.

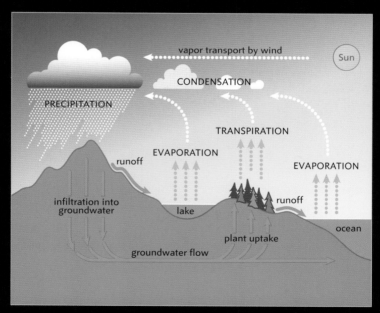

This diagram illustrates the movement of water through the atmosphere, aquifers, and large bodies such as lakes and seas. The GRACE and GRACE-FO missions seek to track all these moving parts of the cycle.

WHY WATER MATTERS

Water is obviously important. Here are three ways water transforms the planet:

- Life depends on water. We have yet to discover life-forms that can exist without it. Even species that can survive extreme conditions need water at some point in their life cycles.
- Water can dissolve more substances than any other liquid, which allows it to hold and transport minerals and other materials that living things need to survive.
- Water has the ability to absorb and retain heat more efficiently than other substances. Because of this, the ocean, which covers about 71 percent of the Earth's surface, moderates the temperature of the entire planet.

However, even the world's most sophisticated instruments cannot detect water underground or measure the exact mass lost from an ice sheet. Researchers needed a different way to measure water on a planetary scale.

MEASURING WATER ON THE MOVE

As satellite technology emerged in the mid-twentieth century, scientists realized that variations in Earth's gravity were altering the orbits of the spacecraft. When a satellite flies over an area with more mass, such as a huge mountain, Earth tugs a little harder. In a flat area near sea level, the pull is weaker. Scientists tweaked satellite orbits to account for these variations, but this solution only fixed part of the problem. The mass of some regions on Earth changed with the seasons. These changes weren't constant over a year, nor were they the same every year, so scientists couldn't account for them in the computer programs that controlled satellite orbits.

Because land moves extremely slowly, except during a massive earthquake or volcanic eruption, scientists realized these seasonal changes in Earth's mass in particular locations were due to shifting water. They speculated that because water's mass—the amount of matter found in each molecule—remains the same, regardless of whether it is vapor, liquid, or solid, it might be possible to track water on Earth by measuring gravitational changes.

By the 1990s, technology had advanced sufficiently to put theory into practice. NASA began work on the Gravity Recovery and Climate Experiment (GRACE) mission with the goal of producing detailed, continuous maps of Earth's gravitational field. Scientists hoped to confirm that maps showing gravity changes on Earth could help track water around the globe. Unlike a typical satellite loaded with sensors and cameras, the twin GRACE satellites themselves were the instruments. One satellite followed the other as they orbited Earth. A microwave beam continually passed between them. As the lead satellite approached an area of greater mass, such as a mountain, gravity tugged a bit harder

PROFILE: PHIL MORTON
PROJECT MANAGER, JET PROPULSION LABORATORY

Phil Morton works on the GRACE and GRACE-FO missions out of NASA's Jet Propulsion Laboratory. He received his BS in electronics engineering from California Polytechnic University. Morton describes the path he took to get to his current job:

"I've always been a builder. I grew up working with every building set you could buy—Lincoln Logs and whatever—and I guess that just kind of continued. Right out of college, I was building video games for four or five years—very early video games. And I got very interested in creative electronics. And somehow I got an offer to come work here at JPL and I thought, well that's pretty spectacular!"

and caused the satellite to speed up. This changed the length of the microwave beam. As the second satellite passed the same spot, it was pulled forward as well, changing the beam length again.

GRACE launched March 17, 2002, and soon after scientists began to assemble charts and visual representations of the world's changing water supply. This is no easy task. The satellites detected changes in beam length as small as a hundredth of the width of a human hair, or about 1 micron. This allowed extremely precise, continual measurements. Data from GRACE consists solely of these measurements, which only show how far apart the two satellites were at any given moment. Researchers have had to create a complex computer program, run by a supercomputer, to help turn raw numbers into useful information.

With this program, the computer first eliminates the effects of atmospheric drag and solar radiation, thanks to measurements from a sensitive accelerometer aboard the satellite. Then the team, with help from the computer, compares variations in one orbit around Earth to previous orbits along the same path. Finally, they look at the satellites' positions relative to the sun and moon, the fluctuation of ocean tides, the position of large weather systems, and the location of known, fixed features, such as mountains and deep oceans. All these things affect the motion of the satellites in known amounts. Once variations from known sources are eliminated, what remains are changes in Earth's gravity that are largely the result of moving water. The scientists use this data to create a diagram that shows how gravity has shifted compared to previous measurements.

LEARNING FROM GRACE

The GRACE mission ended in 2017 after circling Earth every ninety minutes for fifteen years. During that time, GRACE data allowed scientists to map groundwater amounts and locations over the entire globe. These maps indicate that groundwater, or water stored

An artist's rendering of the GRACE satellite instruments in orbit. Earth's gravity tugging on the twin satellites causes the microwave beam passing between them to lengthen or shorten. By tracking the changing beam length, scientists can calculate where and how water moves around the globe.

underground in aquifers, is dwindling rapidly in about one-third of the largest groundwater basins, primarily due to overuse by communities that depend upon them for drinking water, irrigation, and other uses.

GRACE also provided data that allowed scientists to determine the precise sources of sea level rise. From 2005 to 2016, increased ocean mass accounted for about 64 percent of sea level rise. The remaining 36 percent can be attributed to water expanding due to rising ocean temperatures—warmer water simply takes up more space than cooler water. Much of the ocean's increased mass came from melting ice sheets in Greenland and Antarctica. GRACE data revealed that these two massive ice sheets are melting faster than scientists had been able to determine from land-based observations. Over GRACE's fifteen-year mission, Greenland lost about 280 metric gigatons of ice per year and

Antarctica lost nearly 120 metric gigatons a year. GRACE has also shown that melt rates are increasing, meaning that ocean levels will continue to rise around the globe.

To continue these crucial observations, NASA launched the Gravity Recovery and Climate Experiment Follow-On (GRACE-FO) mission on May 22, 2018. The new satellites include improved computer and instrumentation, along with a brand-new instrument—an inter-satellite laser-ranging interferometer. GRACE-FO still uses microwaves for the primary measurements, but the scientists hope the interferometer will make even better measurements—possibly over ten times more precise than the microwave laser. If it works, it will be used as the primary measuring device on future missions.

GRACE and its successor, GRACE-FO, allow scientists to follow water's journey around the globe, from ocean to land and back again. Data show how humans' overconsumption and a changing climate are disrupting the water cycle. Armed with this information, local and national governments and agencies around the world can take action to conserve freshwater supplies and to address climate change, thus protecting the cycle that carries water from the ocean to every corner of the globe.

CHAPTER 2

THE SHAPE OF THE SEA

Earth is a water world—but not a world of water alone. Land interacts with water, sometimes in dramatic ways. On rocky cliffs at Shore Acres State Park near Coos Bay, Oregon, people gather on stormy winter days to see land and water clash with astonishing results. The rocks in the park jut out into the Pacific Ocean at an angle, like tipping towers. When ocean swells reach the shore, they crash into the angled rocks. There is nowhere to go but up, and the resulting waves reach high into the air. The largest ocean swells produce waves over 200 feet (61 m) tall that tower far above the heads of spectators perched on clifftops above.

The waves at Shore Acres are an extreme example of how the ocean's bathymetry—the shape of the seafloor—interacts with the water. Bathymetry includes the depth of the water and the seafloor's topographical features, such as mountains, canyons, hills, and plains. The ocean's bathymetry dictates how water moves, how it interacts with coastal areas, and where and when deep-water nutrients upwell to feed life at the surface. This affects humans in many ways, besides

TECH FOCUS: THE EVOLUTION OF SEAFLOOR MAPPING TECHNOLOGY

Over the last century, scientists and engineers have developed these increasingly sophisticated and accurate tools to map the seafloor:

- Early mapping efforts used lead weights on long ropes to take periodic depth measurements.
- Wire drag surveys, a method developed in the early twentieth century, revealed smaller features, such as large rocks and shipwrecks, which could pose a hazard to ships.
- Developed before World War I, single-beam sonar uses a single, repeating "ping" of sound to measure the distance from the seafloor to the bottom of the ship.
- Multibeam sonar, developed in the 1960s, uses multiple sound waves to build a picture of a swath of the seafloor.
- Multibeam sonar mounted to autonomous surface vehicles (ASVs) allows mapping efforts to cover a wider area than can be accomplished by a single ship.

Though substantially faster and more accurate than dropping a rope, single-beam sonar still only recorded the shape of the seafloor directly under a ship. For large-scale maps needed by navigators and scientists, a better solution was required. The navy developed multibeam sonar in the late 1960s, and NOAA first used it in the late 1970s. It works like a single-beam sonar system, but multiple beams of sound emit from the transducer in a fan shape. A computer program keeps track of the speed and angles of the returning sound signals. It also accounts for the movement of the ship. By combining these data, the program builds up a picture of an area of seafloor that, depending on the ocean depth, can be almost 12 miles (19 km) wide. The resolution of images depends on the depth of the water, but continually improving technology allows for more precision. Smaller features at larger depths are finally becoming visible.

INTO THE DEEP

Sonar systems have continued to advance, with improvements to resolution and the ability to function in both deep and shallow waters. Despite this, only 10 to 15 percent of the ocean has been mapped at resolutions of 300 by 300 feet (100 by 100 m) and only 0.05 percent has been mapped at higher resolutions. Why the delay, when this powerful technology has been available for forty years?

MANY MILES TO GO

This question brings up the second barrier to ocean mapping. The ocean is so large that a single ship outfitted with a multi-beam sonar system would take hundreds of years to map the ocean. Though mapping efforts are not limited to one ship, the ocean is too big, the missions too costly, and the ships too few to fully image the 139 million square miles (361 million sq. km) of Earth's surface that the ocean covers.

Most ships in the world's collective waters stick to a network of well-traveled routes. Detailed maps of the ocean most often cover shipping routes and areas along continental shelves.

To expand our knowledge of the ocean floor, the General Bathymetric Chart of the Oceans, an international organization tasked with mapping the entire ocean floor, has teamed up with the Nippon Foundation to launch Seabed 2030. The project aims to assemble a high-resolution map of the seafloor by 2030. Their first task is collecting all bathymetric information held by public and private entities. Second is compiling data and releasing it to the public so it can be accessed by commercial, recreational, and scientific groups. Seabed 2030 also

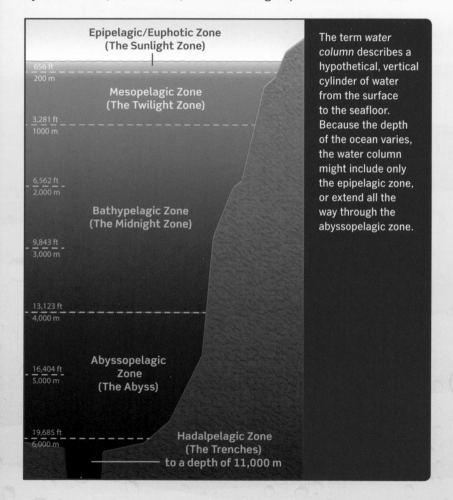

Epipelagic/Euphotic Zone
(The Sunlight Zone)

656 ft
200 m

Mesopelagic Zone
(The Twilight Zone)

3,281 ft
1000 m

6,562 ft
2,000 m

Bathypelagic Zone
(The Midnight Zone)

9,843 ft
3,000 m

13,123 ft
4,000 m

Abyssopelagic
Zone
(The Abyss)

16,404 ft
5,000 m

19,685 ft
6,000 m

Hadalpelagic Zone
(The Trenches)
to a depth of 11,000 m

The term *water column* describes a hypothetical, vertical cylinder of water from the surface to the seafloor. Because the depth of the ocean varies, the water column might include only the epipelagic zone, or extend all the way through the abyssopelagic zone.

hopes to encourage commercial and recreational ocean vessels to carry bathymetric sounding equipment with them, to collect bathymetric readings on trips they plan to undertake anyway.

Even these substantial efforts will only get us part of the way to Seabed 2030's goal. Scientists and engineers hope emerging technology will help us get the rest of the way. At the Center for Coastal and Ocean Mapping/Joint Hydrographic Center, a partnership between NOAA and the University of New Hampshire, scientists and students regularly test several models of autonomous surface vehicles (ASVs). Scientists hope that these robotic boats, which are outfitted with multibeam sonar and communication equipment, will someday be able to team up with ship-based operations to map larger areas of ocean than ships could do alone. These devices, including a bright yellow vehicle nicknamed *BEN* and smaller vehicles dubbed Z-boat and EMILY, cruise Great Bay in New Hampshire. This allows researchers to test everything from the latest survey hardware to updated computer programs.

On the opposite side of the country, researchers from the Monterey Bay Aquarium Research Institute in California test autonomous underwater vehicles (AUVs) equipped with three types of mapping sonars—a multibeam sonar, a sidescan sonar, and a sub-bottom profiler. These vehicles descend up to 3.7 miles (6 km) to map the deep-ocean floor in high resolution. The multibeam sonar creates a detailed image of the seafloor, while the sidescanners provide details about the nature of the surfaces being mapped. This information can combine with data from the multibeam sonar to create three-dimensional images of deep-ocean features, including shipwrecks and downed planes. Finally, the sub-bottom profiler uses sound to penetrate ocean sediments—the layers of mud and decaying material on the seafloor. By sending sound through the sediment layers, scientists can detect hidden geological features, such as layers of different material and fault lines. Repeat mapping of the seafloor allows scientists to see how the floor of a submarine canyon might change. This allows them to determine lava

PROFILE: EMERY NOLASCO

AUV OPERATIONS ENGINEER, MONTEREY BAY AQUARIUM RESEARCH INSTITUTE, CALIFORNIA

Emery Nolasco works with a team at the Monterey Bay Aquarium Research Institute that operates, maintains, and repairs AUVs. Nolasco says that the "majority of our long (10 days to 3-week) missions, since I've joined MBARI, have been seafloor mapping missions. During this time, AUV Operations runs 24/7 with 1 to 2 vehicles.

"When we're not on expeditions, we're maintaining and modifying the vehicles for their next missions. We run a lot of one-day deployments to collect data and test the vehicles. I specialize in mechanical engineering and fabrication, so while we're on shore, I work on designing and fabricating hardware."

Nolasco finds "the tools and systems that are created and developed in oceanography and marine fields" the most exciting things about her work. "These tools can be utilized in and push forward progress in other fields such as space research and exploration. I find it so cool that every launch and recovery feels like the launch of a space ship. We're sending tools out into the unknown, and it takes an incredible effort including a huge team of very versatile skilled people to make it successful."

When asked what she wished people knew about the ocean, Nolasco said, "I wish people could understand the magnitude and immediate effect that the ocean's health has on them. Also, because of how inaccessible the ocean is to the majority of people, I wish they knew what it was like to experience it. There are many moments out at sea that I wish I could capture like how silk-like the ocean looks when it's still, how bright bioluminescent pyrosomes shine when stirred up, and how marine snow looks like stars."

Emery Nolasco and her team members from Monterey Bay Aquarium Research Institute launch an autonomous underwater vehicle (AUV) designed to map the ocean floor.

flow areas and volumes and to monitor the inflation of a volcano toward the next eruption.

Robotic devices are venturing out in sheltered bays under the watchful eyes of humans. Soon they will sail open water, creating detailed images of the hidden ocean. The ocean's vast depth and immense size has kept its bathymetry concealed for all of human history. A complete, high-resolution map of the ocean is becoming a reality, through the determination of scientists and engineers, with the support of such people as technicians, database managers, philanthropists, and commercial and private sailors. New maps created with the latest technology may reveal hidden habitats and geology that could be rich sources of oil and natural gas, minerals, and food. Whether humans will use this new knowledge to exploit the ocean's resources or safeguard them remains to be seen.

THE SHAPE OF THE SEA

CHAPTER 3

WHAT GOES AROUND
COMES AROUND

On January 10, 1992, rough seas in the North Pacific tossed around a container ship bound for Tacoma, Washington. Twelve containers tumbled overboard during the storm. At least one broke open, releasing packages of plastic bath toys: red beavers, blue turtles, green frogs, and yellow ducks. The packaging was no match for the relentless waves. Within hours, about 28,800 toys escaped and were free to sail the high seas.

Ten months later, beachcombers in the islands of southeast Alaska, near Sitka, began to find hundreds of the toys. Bath toys continued to turn up in southeast Alaska for years after the accident, several years apart. Word of the incident's continuing fallout reached Curtis Ebbesmeyer, a scientist studying ocean currents and their effect on ocean debris, and Jim Ingraham, a scientist working to develop the Ocean Surface Current Simulator. They set out to follow the bobbing bath toys in their journeys around the ocean.

Like Georg von Neumayer's "message in a bottle" study in the nineteenth century, tracking the bath toys and other objects lost at sea has helped Ebbesmeyer and Ingraham chart current patterns around the world.

The work of Ebbesmeyer and Ingraham showed that the toys were entrained in the North Pacific Subpolar Gyre. This circular current runs west from the Aleutians, where the accident occurred, to Japan, and then back east toward southeast Alaska. As the toys made the loop, dozens continued to wash ashore each year.

Ocean currents result from the influence of wind, tides, energy from the sun, differences in water density, and the rotation of Earth. The shape of the coasts and the seafloor affects the location, direction, and speed of currents. These elements produce local and large-scale patterns that are reliable and predictable. But within these patterns, variations exist. These variations are the reason that at least one duck and one frog escaped the North Pacific Subpolar Gyre, traveled through the Bering Strait, and floated into the Arctic Ocean. Frozen in pack ice, the pair made it all the way to the North Atlantic Ocean. The duck showed up in Maine, while the frog made landfall in Scotland. Three other toys—a turtle, a beaver, and a frog— hopped the North Pacific Subtropical Gyre to the Hawaiian Islands.

MOVING WATER
AROUND THE GLOBE

Adventuring bath toys provide insight into the patterns of moving water that impact human activities around the globe. Because more than 90 percent of international trading of goods is done by sea, understanding currents is vital for planning the fastest, most efficient way to move goods from one port to another. Knowledge of currents also informs weather predictions and relief effort responses to disasters such as oil spills. Most important, currents influence the global climate. The ocean absorbs most of the solar radiation that reaches Earth. However, this heat energy isn't evenly distributed. More energy from the sun reaches the equator than the poles. Currents take the energy soaked up by water near the equator and move it toward the poles. So places such as Anchorage, Alaska, and Oslo, Norway, are much milder and more habitable than they would be without the ocean's influence.

Surface currents—the ones that ferried the various bath toys around the globe—are largely driven by wind. Deep ocean currents are driven by temperature and salinity (level of salt) in a thermohaline circulation. *Thermo* refers to heat, and *haline* refers to salt. Heat and salt influence the density of the water. Colder and saltier water is denser. It will sink below warmer and less salty water. When denser water sinks, less dense water moves in to take its place. This thermohaline circulation partners with wind patterns to drive a current known as the ocean conveyer belt. This system moves heat energy around the globe and brings nutrients up from the deep ocean, sustaining ocean food webs. From the North Atlantic, cold, dense water sinks and flows south. It circles the Antarctic continent and then moves up toward the Indian and Pacific Oceans. As heat mixes downward, the deep water rises. It travels past Indonesia, around Africa, up the Atlantic, and back to the North Atlantic.

Of course, it's not really quite as simple as the diagram implies. Global systems and patterns do exist, but within any given region, the actual ocean circulation patterns are much more complex and

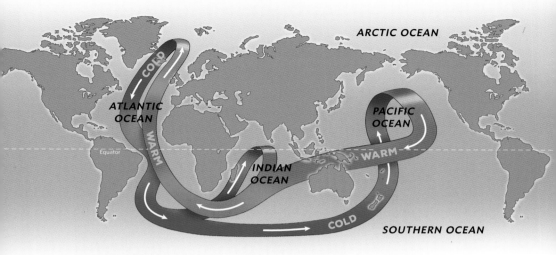

The above graphic illustrates part of the global circulation of warm water (indicated with red) and cooler water (indicated with blue).

nuanced. It's a lot like patterns in the atmosphere. Jet streams impact global weather by moving warm and cool air masses around the globe. Smaller low- and high-pressure systems at lower altitudes also cause winds and move clouds on a regional scale. Finally, some winds and precipitation move at a local level. All these systems and layers interact with one another in complex ways. The same is true in the ocean. Global current patterns interact with regional patterns, which interact with local patterns down to multitudes of tiny, swirling eddies no bigger than a toy boat. In the deep ocean, water of different densities forms layers. Untangling the nuances of how all these patterns interact with one another is vital to understanding how complexities and variations in one region affect the global pattern as a whole.

An example of a regional system within the global pattern occurs in the Atlantic Ocean. Water moves northward through the Straits of Florida, transporting heat energy along the eastern coast of North America and into the North Atlantic. When this wind-driven, warm-water current—the Gulf Stream—reaches the North Atlantic, it cools, releasing heat into the atmosphere. The cooler, denser water sinks into the deep ocean. It circulates in the North Atlantic and then makes its way south.

Heat energy carried by ocean currents moderates temperatures in such places as England, making winters there about 18°F (10°C) warmer than other places at the same latitude.

This circulation system, known as the Atlantic Meridional Overturning Circulation (AMOC), is vital to the global ocean circulation. It pulls warm surface waters northward in the Atlantic and drives the southward movement of deep water from the Arctic to the Antarctic. This flow is important for maintaining a stable climate. Past changes to this pattern may have contributed to dramatic climate change. Scientists are concerned that impacts to the AMOC due to a warming climate could have consequences we don't yet fully understand. Computer-based climate models predict that that AMOC will slow in the future. Scientists need real-world data over an extended time to confirm or disprove this projection.

TAKING THE OCEAN'S "PULSE"

In 2004 ocean scientists with the RAPID Climate Change project deployed a newly developed array of sensors at latitude 26° north. The row of twenty-four moorings stretches from the Canary Islands near the African coast, over the mid-Atlantic ridge, and to the Bahamas off the coast of North America. Sensors mounted at different depths on each mooring survey temperature, electrical conductivity (from which scientists calculate salinity), and pressure along the entire water column. Near the Bahamas, scientists also deployed instruments that measure current speed and direction. The instruments take readings every hour for about eighteen months. Then the researchers retrieve the array, download data, and redeploy the sensors.

Scientists use the pressure, salinity, and temperature data collected by the array to calculate density at different depths. Deep-water currents are driven by differences in density because dense water wants to sink and less dense water wants to rise. However, because Earth is rotating, when the dense water moves under the less dense water, it turns clockwise (in the Northern Hemisphere). When the RAPID data indicates denser water at the same depth near the Bahamas as compared to the Canary Islands, scientists know southward flow is occurring at this depth. They use data about east-west density differences to calculate the movement of water northward and southward along the array. Near the Bahamas, researchers also use current speed and direction data to determine the amount of water transported north by the Gulf Stream. Combined, the density and velocity data allows scientists to calculate the rate of overturning, or "the amount of water going north at shallow depths, and the equal amount of water going south at greater depths."

DOUBLE AND TRIPLE CHECKING

When scientists state something with reasonable certainty, it's because test after test, study after study, has confirmed the results. Good scientists never rely on the results from a single study to draw a definitive conclusion. They also rely on the work of other scientists who use different research tools. For example, when scientists working on the GRACE mission (chapter 1) detected changes in the AMOC, they compared their findings to data collected by the RAPID arrays. RAPID data confirmed the changes detected with the GRACE satellites.

PROFILE: ELEANOR FRAJKA-WILLIAMS

PRINCIPAL RESEARCH SCIENTIST, NATIONAL OCEANOGRAPHY CENTRE, SOUTHAMPTON, UNITED KINGDOM

Eleanor Frajka-Williams is an observational physical oceanographer at the National Oceanography Centre in the UK. Her work encompasses making "measurements (observations) of the real oceans to try to deduce variability in circulation (physics) of the ocean, and its causes and impacts."

During a typical day, she generally does "a lot of work at a computer, either programming code to analyze data, or writing reports. In the field, everything is different. We'll typically work 8–10 hour shifts and oversee the instrumentation that we're using to make measurements, checking that everything is working and planning where to make measurements to maximize the value of our time at sea. This can be as exciting as standing on the back deck of a moving ship with the rails down (no barrier to the water) and installing sensors onto long wires to be deployed in the deep ocean, or [as quiet as doing] more computer work as we monitor data quality in real time."

Frajka-Williams says, "I'd really like to know—quantitatively— what role the oceans play in setting the pace of climate change, or setting the patterns of regional climate variability. This is a really complex problem since there are so many interactions in play: between the oceans and the atmosphere, or between the oceans and cryosphere, and even the oceans influence on biology and chemistry. My field of work is not in geoengineering or building solutions to remove carbon from the atmosphere, but I hope that by studying how the ocean responds to and sets the pace of climate change . . . the work I do will help build solutions to the problem of anthropogenic climate change."

MONITORING THE AMOC FROM NORTH TO SOUTH

To expand monitoring in the Atlantic, the North Atlantic Changes array began operations at latitude 47° north in 2006. Farther north, the Overturning in the Subpolar North Atlantic Program (OSNAP) deployed an array from Scotland to Greenland to Canada from 2014 to 2016. Farther south, arrays stretch across the Atlantic at 16° north, 11° south, and 34.5° south. Each data point collected by these ocean-wide monitoring stations helps paint a better picture of the changing currents throughout the sea.

The RAPID team has collected data from the array for about sixteen years, which have revealed a few surprises. Prior to the study, scientists relied on ship-based surveys that provided infrequent snapshots of the rate of overturning. RAPID data revealed much more variation—sometimes the rate of overturning slowed much more than expected and then bounced back. The RAPID team also discovered that the rate of overturning changed seasonally, with more water circulating in the spring and less in the fall. Most significantly, the team has found that the rate of overturning is declining overall.

The exact implications of this decline are unknown. Some studies have shown that changes to the AMOC triggered the Little Ice Age—a period of increased glaciation worldwide and cooler temperatures in the Northern Hemisphere that occurred from about 1300 CE to the late nineteenth century. Newer studies have shown the opposite. Some research seems to indicate that the current slowing of the AMOC is due to climate change, while other studies indicate that it started much earlier. This uncertainty is not surprising, given the complexity of ocean currents and the number of variables involved. The knowledge we have gained so far underscores how much we have yet to learn. The work of the RAPID team and others helps us better understand the impact of currents on the planet's climate.

CHAPTER 4
STORIES TOLD BY WATER

One of water's unique qualities is its ability to dissolve more substances than any other liquid. A body of water's chemistry depends upon the substances it contains. It can contain various amounts of salt, calcium, oxygen, carbon dioxide, and many other chemicals. Scientists "read" stories told by water with instruments that measure its chemical makeup.

The chemistry of the water affects its physical properties. For example, saltier water is denser and tends to sink, pushing less salty water toward the surface. This movement creates upwellings and currents. The chemistry of water also impacts ocean life. Most organisms evolved to live within a specific range of chemical conditions. Extreme changes to water's chemistry threaten ocean-dwelling species and the people who depend on them for food and jobs.

One stark consequence of changing ocean chemistry occurred off the Oregon coast in 2002. Crabbers phoned state fish and wildlife offices to report traps (or pots) full of dead crabs. Scientist Francis Chan sampled the water in areas where crabbers noticed die-offs. Test results told the story—oxygen levels in the affected areas were extremely low. While fishes and other highly mobile animals were able to escape the low-oxygen areas, slow-moving creatures such as crabs and sea stars, as well as stationary life such as mussels and barnacles, suffocated. When the oxygen returned, the fishes did too, but marine invertebrates were slower to bounce back. Across the Northwest, crabbing operations faced uncertainty. When they pulled up their crab pots, would their catch be alive or dead?

In offshore waters in the Pacific Northwest, where the continental shelf ends and ocean depths plunge, low oxygen, or hypoxia, is normal. However, low oxygen conditions had never been reported this close to shore. Initially, scientists thought areas of hypoxia might be a local phenomenon brought on by unusual conditions in a single season. But the hypoxia began to return, year after year. Sometimes it only affected a few square miles. Other years the "dead zones" covered thousands of square miles. In 2006 low oxygen levels persisted for four months. Oxygen levels approached zero in many areas, leaving the seafloor littered with dead sea life. For almost two decades the pattern has continued. In 2018 the low-oxygen event started in early June and didn't abate until early September.

Across the region, the seafood industry and scientists ask the same question: Why? The answer appears to be that the normal pattern is changing. In the summer, winds blow south along the coast of British Columbia, Canada and the states of Washington and Oregon. These winds, along with the rotation of the planet, drive surface water away from the shore. As warm surface waters move toward the open ocean, nutrient-rich but oxygen-poor water upwells from the ocean floor. This upwelling is essential for healthy marine ecosystems. The nutrients power phytoplankton blooms (a "bloom" is the rapid growth of phytoplankton population when conditions are favorable). The blooms are the base of the ocean food web and provide food for thousands of species. As the blooms fade, the dead phytoplankton sink to the ocean bottom, where decomposers get to work. The decomposers consume oxygen as they feed on decaying organic matter. This reduces oxygen levels near the seafloor.

This cycle is a regular occurrence. The phytoplankton blooms fuel one of the most productive fisheries in the world. However, in the fifty years scientists had recorded observations, they had never seen such low dissolved oxygen levels at depths around 165 feet (50 m). Scientists thought many factors might be at play. Ocean temperatures are rising because of global warming. A warmer ocean holds less oxygen. Wind patterns may be changing, probably due to climate change, and a warming ocean may be altering currents. And warmer surface water may be acting like a blanket, keeping the colder water from mixing with other layers. Scientists weren't completely certain. They needed more data—a lot more data.

A NEW WAY TO COLLECT DATA

Scientists could acquire the information they needed by heading out on boats. However, ship time is expensive, and continuous monitoring by scientists aboard a ship is impractical, especially during severe weather and most of the winter. Another option was to use data collected by

HOW HYPOXIA HAPPENS

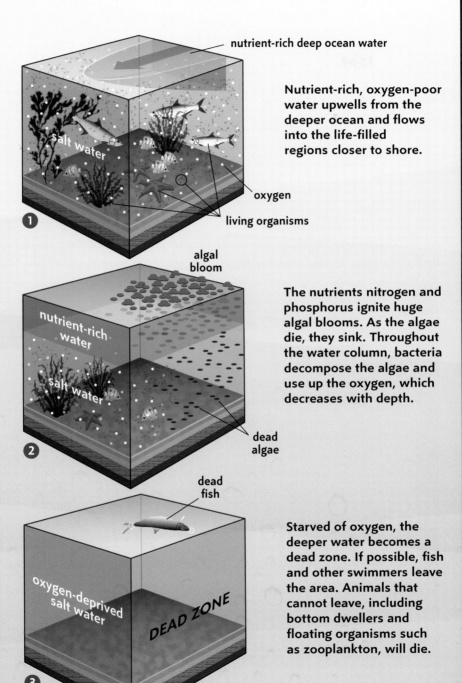

nutrient-rich deep ocean water

salt water

oxygen

living organisms

❶

Nutrient-rich, oxygen-poor water upwells from the deeper ocean and flows into the life-filled regions closer to shore.

algal bloom

nutrient-rich water

salt water

dead algae

❷

The nutrients nitrogen and phosphorus ignite huge algal blooms. As the algae die, they sink. Throughout the water column, bacteria decompose the algae and use up the oxygen, which decreases with depth.

dead fish

oxygen-deprived salt water

DEAD ZONE

❸

Starved of oxygen, the deeper water becomes a dead zone. If possible, fish and other swimmers leave the area. Animals that cannot leave, including bottom dwellers and floating organisms such as zooplankton, will die.

HYPOXIA'S BIGGER, "BADDER" COMPANION

Oxygen levels are not the only "story" water chemistry tests reveal, and growing low-oxygen zones aren't the only changing water condition in the ocean. The ocean naturally absorbs carbon dioxide, so as levels have risen in the atmosphere, the ocean has taken up more CO_2. Water with higher CO_2 levels is more acidic. The average ocean pH levels have dropped from 8.2 to 8.1 over the past two hundred years. This may not sound like much, but it means that ocean water is on average 30 percent more acidic.

Lower pH levels reduce the availability of calcium carbonate in seawater. Without this mineral, animals including clams, oysters, and certain species of zooplankton—such as pteropods (sea butterflies)—cannot build their shells. Because so many other organisms depend on zooplankton for food, the potential collapse of their populations threatens the entire ocean food web. Acidification has already devastated oyster producers on the West Coast of the United States. And coral reefs stressed by warming oceans are unable to replace dead or dying reef structure efficiently. This, in turn, impacts fishing communities dependent on reef fishing and raises the potential for devastating wave damage during storms.

Mike Devin tests the acid levels in the Gulf of Maine. Devin is a marine biologist and legislator from Newcastle, Maine. He believes that state governments have the power necessary to address the effects of ocean acidification. His dual role as a scientist and a politician give him a unique and informed perspective on the issue of climate change.

arrays mounted to moorings that stretch out east of Newport, Oregon, but those sensors are bound to one place. To survey a larger area, scientists turned to a technology that can move through the water, collecting data as it travels—the AUV.

In 2005 scientists from Oregon State University deployed a prototype of a type of AUV called an undersea glider. The seven-foot-long (2 m) glider looks like a brightly painted torpedo. This shape, along with a pair of slender fins, allows the glider to cut through the water. Instead of propellers, the glider uses changes in buoyancy to move through the water.

Sonar equipment detects the glider's depth and keeps it from banging into the seafloor. When it nears bottom, a fluid-filled bladder deflates, decreasing the glider's density. This causes the glider to rise to the surface. As it rises, it measures temperature, salinity, oxygen and light levels, phytoplankton levels, suspended particle concentrations, and dissolved organic material. Scientists can also see if the glider has shifted off its programmed course during its underwater travels. If it has, they can then calculate the strength of currents that pushed the glider off course.

When the glider surfaces every six hours, it relays data it collects to a computer onshore by a satellite phone in its tail. It does this

HOW BUOYANCY PROPELS A GLIDER

Buoyancy is determined by density. An object that is less dense than water will float. One that is denser than water will sink. An object's density is determined by its mass and volume. A glider's mass stays the same, but its volume—the amount of space it takes up in the water—can be changed by adding or subtracting fluid from a bladder in the base of the machine. When fluid is added, the glider's density increases and it begins to sink. Because of its fins, it doesn't sink like a stone. Instead, it sails through the water the same way a sailplane flies through the air.

continuously for about three months. Then the research team installs new batteries in the glider and performs any needed maintenance.

Since the first glider deployment, the team at Oregon State University has added to its fleet and now uses nine gliders. The gliders logged 51,027 miles (82,120 km) between April 2006 and November 2014. They have continued to operate since. Though they travel slowly, only 0.5 nautical miles (0.6 miles, or 0.9 km) per hour, they have saved millions of dollars and have provided scientists with continuous data for fifteen years. The team has gone on to deploy gliders from Washington State, northwestern California, Chile, and many other locations around the world. Newer gliders also carry acoustic monitors. These allow scientists to map ocean currents from the ocean floor to the surface.

INTO THE DEEP

Using data from the gliders as well as fixed and buoy-based sensors, scientists have mapped locations and sizes of low-oxygen zones, including the Pacific Northwest dead zone in 2006, which measured 1,158 square miles (3,000 sq. km)—about the size of Rhode Island. They have confirmed that unlike other parts of the world, where dead zones are driven by run offs of fertilizer and other chemicals, the phenomenon in the Pacific Northwest is driven by upwelling closer to shore than normal.

According to scientists, the cause is climate change. Rising temperatures, changes in wind and current patterns, and increased CO_2 levels have altered the normal low-oxygen cycle just enough to render it

CITIZEN SCIENTISTS ON THE JOB

As scientists on the Oregon coast work to understand changing ocean conditions, they are recruiting members of the community to help. Francis Chan, a professor at Oregon State University, works with volunteers to monitor ocean pH levels. They helped Chan choose the best intertidal locations to mount sensors that monitor ocean pH levels. From spring to fall, the volunteers collect the monitoring stations every four weeks and send them to Chan. After downloading data, Chan installs a new sensor in the monitor and sends it back to the volunteer, who redeploys it for a new round of data gathering.

Oregon crabbers will also be assisting scientists in a new grant from the NOAA Coastal Hypoxia Research Program. Working with scientists from Oregon State University, crabbers will help deploy about forty dissolved oxygen sensors on their crab pots from April to August. As Oregon congressional representative Suzanne Bonamici said, "Strong research partnerships like the work being done at Oregon State University will help improve our understanding of hypoxia and ocean health, giving affected communities the tools they need to adapt and mitigate the effects."

Oyster farms along the Pacific Coast of the United States were among the first to feel the effects of climate change. As ocean water becomes more acidic, it prevents tiny oyster larvae from forming shells. Without these larval or "seed" oysters, farmers cannot replenish their beds for future harvests.

deadly to ocean life. Warmer surface temperatures inhibit the mixing of ocean layers, which normally increase oxygen levels deeper down. And the upwelling cold, oxygen-poor water contains even less oxygen than it would have in the past due to this upper-ocean warming and changes in ocean circulation. Scientists continue to track conditions to understand all the variables.

For crabbers in Oregon pulling up pots of dead crabs, climate change is not a "what if" scenario—it is their reality. Hypoxia along with acidification and rising temperatures are actively affecting the chemistry of ocean water around the globe and negatively impacting people who depend on the ocean for life and livelihood. By monitoring hypoxia and acidification with a huge range of technologies, scientists continually gather more precise data to pinpoint the causes and behavior of these phenomena. Though this knowledge will not stop the changes to the ocean's upwelling cycles, understanding the big picture may help seafood producers on the West Coast adapt to these new conditions.

PART 2
THE LIVING OCEAN

CHAPTER 5

THE BEGINNING OF LIFE AND BREATH

Nearly every life-form in the sea connects to every other through the pelagic, or open ocean, food web. The primary producers in this community are the phytoplankton, most of which cannot be seen without a microscope. Like plants on land, phytoplankton use the sun's energy to create food for themselves. This energy passes to zooplankton, the primary consumers, which in turn passes to larger invertebrates, fishes, and mammals that are secondary and tertiary consumers. Everything dies and the decomposition process releases nutrients back into the system. This web of life is powered by the sun, even in the deepest parts of the sea.

Off the coast of South America, where Peru curves southeast to meet Chile, an occasional upwelling brings cool, nutrient-rich water to the sunlit surface. This sudden bonanza gives phytoplankton ingredients they need to reproduce rapidly. In twenty-four hours, the "bloom" has increased to hundreds of square miles.

This explosion of life kicks the ocean food web into high gear. First to benefit are other members of the plankton community. Unicellular zooplankton, such as radiolarians and foraminifera, devour the phytoplankton. Other zooplankton species—the larvae of larger ocean animals such as crabs, lobsters, and fishes—join the feast. Then massive schools of small fishes—sardines or anchovies—begin to arrive, attracting larger predators. Huge groups of dolphins work together to trap the fish

This satellite photo captures an immense phytoplankton bloom that stretches for 500 miles (805 km) off the coast of Brazil. While the dark green swirls make up a single bloom, the lighter green clouds close to the shore may belong to a different bloom or consist of sediments stirred up by recent flooding.

NO SUN REQUIRED

Most deep-ocean ecosystems ultimately rely on energy from the sun that makes its way to the ocean floor as detritus. One ecosystem, however, does not require the sun at all—underwater geysers called hydrothermal vents. Mineral-rich water gushing from these features has been superheated by magma under the ocean's crust. Extreme pressure at this depth prevents it from becoming steam. The hottest hydrothermal vents spew water up to 750°F (400°C).

Despite these harsh conditions, life thrives here. At the base of a hydrothermal vent food web are microscopic "extremophiles"—species of bacteria and archaea that can survive these superheated conditions. Instead of photosynthesis, these life-forms rely on chemosynthesis, the process of converting chemicals in the superheated water into food energy. Animals such as limpets and shrimp feed on the microorganisms. Larger creatures such as tube worms, crabs, and even octopuses thrive here as well. Chemosynthetic life also forms the base of food webs in other inhospitable places such as deep caves and hot springs, as well as on shipwrecks and whale carcasses.

against the ocean surface and then pick them off one by one. Sharks and other large fishes join the feeding frenzy. Birds flying overhead dive into the waves to grab a share. Fishing boats bobbing on the surface cast their nets into the fray.

The bloom finishes its life cycle in just a few days. The crowds disperse and head off to find their next meal. Any remaining phytoplankton die and begin to sink to the ocean floor, feeding organisms all the way down the water column. The life cycle of phytoplankton impacts ocean life from sunlit surface zones to canyons so deep light cannot reach. But the influence of phytoplankton extends beyond their role as food. It's not just ocean dwellers who depend on them.

GIVING OXYGEN, TAKING CARBON

The term *phytoplankton* applies to a variety of photosynthetic plankton organisms. Two large groups of phytoplankton are cyanobacteria and protists. Cyanobacteria, like all bacteria, are prokaryotes and lack cell nuclei. They use specialized membranes to carry out photosynthesis. Protists are single-celled eukaryotes. Unlike bacteria, they possess one or more nuclei and complex organelles. They carry out photosynthesis in their chloroplasts, just as land plants do. The variety found among protists species is astonishing. For example, species of coccolithophores surround themselves with calcium carbonate scales. Dinoflagellates protect themselves with cellulose-based "armor" and motor through the

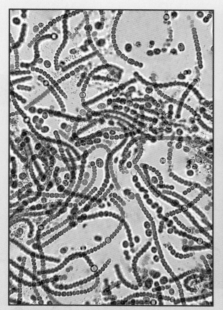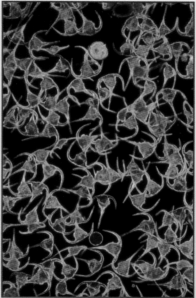

Above are two microscope images showing two different kinds of phytoplankton: cyanobacteria (*left*) and dinoflagellates (*right*). The main feature all plankton have in common is that they drift with the currents. Some creatures are permanent members of the plankton community. Larvae of fishes, crustaceans, cephalopods, and other groups are temporary members, leaving when they gain the ability to swim against the currents.

water with two waving appendages called flagella. Diatoms manufacture exquisite silica structures. And these are just some of the many different shapes that protists can take.

TINY CLOUD MAKERS

What with being the base of the ocean food web, producing about half the planet's oxygen, and regulating atmospheric carbon, phytoplankton, it would seem, couldn't handle one more role. But it turns out they might also influence cloud formation over the open ocean.

Clouds are made up of tiny water droplets that have condensed from water vapor. At the center of each droplet is a tiny particle, or nucleus, usually made of dust, pollen, or some other microscopic solid. Without a nucleus, it is much harder for water droplets, and by extension clouds, to form. When more nuclei are available, more droplets form. Clouds play an important role in reflecting sunlight away from the planet's surface. The more droplets a cloud contains, the more sunlight is reflected back into space. This cools the planet below.

Scientists studying cloud formation in the Southern Ocean found that more cloud droplets exist over areas with higher concentrations of phytoplankton. Apparently, plankton are one source of particles that become cloud condensation nuclei. Plankton release gases into the air when their cells age or when they are eaten. These gases combine with other particles to form microscopic solids.

Sea spray may also facilitate the movement of organic particles—bits of life-forms such as plankton, bacteria, and viruses—into the atmosphere. These particles may provide additional nuclei for droplet formation. More studies are needed to understand the exact role phytoplankton and other microscopic ocean life play in the formation of clouds. But this may be one more way that tiny denizens of the ocean drive the fundamental cogs of the climate machine.

As a group, phytoplankton contribute about 50 percent of Earth's total annual oxygen production—as much as the vast prairies, dense forests, and sweltering jungles on land combined. Diatoms alone are so numerous that scientists estimate they contribute about half of the total oxygen output of all phytoplankton, or a quarter of Earth's total annual production of oxygen.

Phytoplankton also play a vital role in Earth's carbon cycle. Carbon dioxide from the atmosphere dissolves in the water at the ocean's

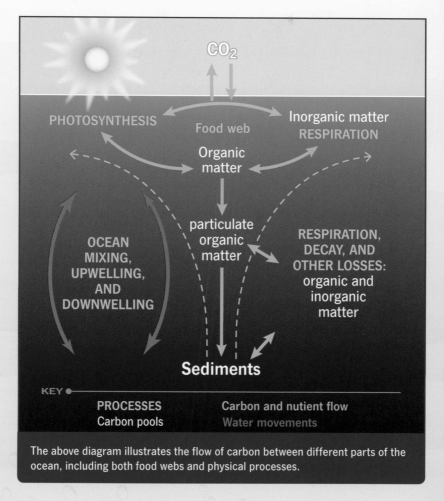

The above diagram illustrates the flow of carbon between different parts of the ocean, including both food webs and physical processes.

surface. Phytoplankton use the carbon during photosynthesis. When phytoplankton die and begin to decompose, some of this carbon is released, but some is sequestered, or contained, in the remains that begin to sink toward the ocean floor.

When an organism eats the phytoplankton or its remains, the carbon passes to the next level of the food web. Some is exhaled or excreted. Some stays within the animal. When another animal eats the first, the carbon is passed along. So carbon makes its way through the food web, passing from one organism to the next. As it is continuously eaten and eaten again, carbon also makes its way deeper into the ocean. Though most carbon eventually makes its way back into the ocean and the atmosphere, some of the carbon ends up in sediments on the ocean floor. The carbon tied up in the ocean food web and in ocean floor sediments can remain sequestered for a long time. Sequestering prevents carbon from circulating back into the atmosphere. This has had and continues to have an impact on Earth's climate by removing carbon from the atmosphere, thus slowing the greenhouse effect.

A VOYAGE OF DISCOVERY

We know that phytoplankton affect the planet in ways that far exceed their diminutive sizes. But like our knowledge of other areas of oceanography, we have huge holes in our understanding of these organisms. We don't even know how many species there are, how they are genetically related to one another, and how they interact with other members of the plankton community. Fully comprehending the role phytoplankton play in Earth's climate will be impossible until we have a better understanding of the players involved.

In 2009 the schooner *Tara* set off from Lorient, France, to embark on a study of plankton. The goal of the Tara Oceans mission was to sail all the world's oceans, sampling and cataloging marine plankton along the way. The visual, numerical, and genetic information collected would create a reference data set for scientists around the globe.

TECH FOCUS: FLOW IMAGING MICROSCOPE

A flow imaging microscope's unique combinations of microfluidics, laser detector, camera, and computer allow it to image and categorize thousands of organisms quickly. It's the machine's microfluidics—the ability to achieve extremely small streams of fluids—that distinguishes it from other microscopes.

This was a daunting task, given that a single gallon (3.8 L) of water can contain thousands of organisms representing dozens of species. Samples were taken from multiple depths along with water chemistry readings. Scientists carefully sorted the organisms for further study. To help them quickly assess the population makeup and density in certain samples, they brought along a flow imaging microscope—a combination of a microscope, a camera, a laser, and a computer program able to record specific data points for each organism photographed. It can detect all but the smallest organisms, so Tara Oceans researchers used it to catalog any plankton larger than bacteria.

To begin the analysis, an operator places a small sample of ocean water into the machine. Then a tiny microsyringe pump pulls a thin stream of water through a tube and in front of the camera. The laser senses when an object passes by the screen, which triggers the camera to take an image. As the camera rapidly feeds images to the computer, the computer records data about each image. One by one, the enlarged images of each organism pop up on the screen.

The computer program associated with the microscope allows the scientists to look at all the images together or group them by different parameters. For example, a researcher can look at all the organisms that fall within a specific size range or view organisms that share a similar shape. Using the flow imaging microscope, scientists can catalog the density and diversity of life in a given sample much

© Sarah Fretwell /

Flora Vincent folds polycarbonate filters used to analyze viral communities. Viruses are part of the planktonic ecosystem.

more quickly than by hand. They can also use the images to create a database that can be used by scientists studying other aspects of phytoplankton communities.

During the expedition's 1,140 days, 160 scientists collected more than thirty-five thousand plankton samples from the ocean's surface down to a depth of 3,281 feet (1,000 m). Images collected by the flow imaging microscope allowed scientists to assess the diversity of larger organisms in specific locations. They combined this information with

INTO THE DEEP

PROFILE: FLORA VINCENT

POSTDOCTORAL RESEARCHER, VARDI LAB, WEIZMANN INSTITUTE OF SCIENCE, ISRAEL

Scientist Flora Vincent studies how interactions between organisms affect evolution of life in the ocean. She used data collected by Tara Oceans to identify a newly discovered partnership between species of photosynthetic diatoms and zooplankton called tintinnid ciliates. The evidence she and other scientists gathered indicates that the tintinnids derive protection from the diatoms' rigid exoskeletons. The diatoms, in turn, gain increased movement thanks to the tintinnids' whirring cilia—the tiny, hairlike organelles that propel the organism through the water.

Vincent says the most exciting part of her work is "that we're pushing boundaries of what we know about life in the ocean. It's exciting because it's a lot about exploration (both in the field and in front of my computer)." She says that "marine microbiology is in this amazing era. . . . We're looking at tiny microorganisms that impact the whole planet including us—this is fascinating."

data collected by sensors that measured different aspects of water chemistry, as well as their more detailed examinations of sampled organisms across all size ranges. They determined that temperature had a noticeable effect on the presence of certain bacteria species. This discovery suggests that warming oceans will affect these invisible ocean communities. We don't yet know exactly how this will influence the amount of oxygen phytoplankton produce or how much carbon they take up. Clearly, disruptions to phytoplankton cycles could significantly disrupt the rest of life on Earth.

Tara Oceans scientists have helped us fill in the gaps of our knowledge about phytoplankton. But probably many species haven't been discovered. Just as the immensity of the ocean presents barriers to oceanographers attempting to map the seafloor, follow currents, or chart changes in ocean chemistry, the vastness of the sea also makes it difficult to study individual life-forms, especially those effectively invisible to our eyes. Communities of phytoplankton, with their outsized influence on the planet, demand our attention. To understand them is to understand better the world in which we live—and the world of the future.

CHAPTER 6

LIFE IN A DROP

Scoop a cup of seawater from the ocean and place a single drop on a microscope slide. Chances are good the sample teems with life. The drop likely harbors viruses, bacteria, and phytoplankton. It might also contain zooplankton, the primary consumers in the ocean food web.

Zooplankton are eukaryotic organisms—life-forms whose cells have nuclei—that do not photosynthesize and that generally drift with ocean currents. Zooplankton range from single-cell life-forms, such as species of tintinnids and foraminifera, to siphonophores, whose colonies can exceed 90 feet (27 m) in length. Many zooplankton drift in the plankton community throughout their lives. Others—the embryos and larvae of fishes, crabs, lobsters, shrimp, sea urchins, and many other creatures—are part of the plankton community until they are large and strong enough to swim against the currents or, in some cases, settle to the ocean floor.

TINY "STIR STICKS"

Recent studies show that zooplankton's movement up and down the water column, particularly during diel vertical migration, might contribute to the mixing of ocean layers. Though each creature only moves a miniscule amount of water individually, collectively these creatures may actually "stir" the ocean and transfer nutrients from one ocean layer to another.

In the waters of Alaska, a species of copepod called *Neocalanus flemingeri* helps sustain the largest fishing industry in the United States. These copepods have a life cycle that allows them to survive long, cold northern winters. In late winter and early spring, *Neocalanus flemingeri* eggs hatch. The larvae, called nauplii, migrate to the surface to feed on the spring phytoplankton bloom. They eat, grow, and molt until they finally reach the copepodite stage. Then they are nearly adults. They continue to feed, trying to store as much fat in their bodies as possible to sustain themselves over the long winter. By midsummer the blooms have passed. The copepodites descend to about 1,300 to 1,800 feet (400 to 550 m) below the surface, where they will molt one last time. After the final molt is complete, the adults stop eating and begin looking for mates.

After mating, the males die. Females enter a state called diapause, similar to hibernation, when growth and development ceases, and metabolism slows. As Alaska's short summer ends and winter descends, the females rest. With luck, they have put on enough fat to carry them through their fall and early winter "naps." In midwinter they rouse and their bodies begin to produce eggs. They lay up to one thousand eggs over a four- to six-week period, and the cycle begins all over again.

The life cycle of this species, as well as the food chains that depend on them, relies on the timing of the annual phytoplankton bloom. Because their life cycle takes a full year, a small or abnormally timed phytoplankton bloom one year may lead to a copepod population crash the next. As climate change transforms ocean cycles and impacts the timing and strength of phytoplankton blooms, scientists are working to understand how populations of copepods are adapting.

READING A CELL'S MESSAGES

To assess how copepods are coping with changing environmental conditions, scientists need to understand what is happening inside the animal's body during different parts of its life cycle. They can then use that information to understand how changing conditions affect each stage of the life cycle. But how do you peek inside the inner workings of an animal so small that it can barely be seen with the naked eye? A team at the University of Hawai'i at Mānoa, led by Professor Petra H. Lenz,

Vittoria Roncalli sorts *Neocalanus flemingeri* individuals from a sample collected in the field.

uses a number of new techniques, including one called transcriptomics, to solve this problem.

Transcriptomics is the study of ribonucleic acid (RNA) molecules in a cell. It has revolutionized biology because it allows scientists to have a better understanding of what is happing in a cell, a tissue, and even an entire organism based on gene sequences currently active in the cells.

An easy way to think of it is this: deoxyribonucleic acid (DNA) is like a recipe book containing all the instructions needed to create and operate an organism. Messenger RNA (mRNA), the RNA active in a cell at any given time, copies a single recipe from the DNA and carries it from the cell nucleus to the "chef," a ribosome. It then makes a protein using instructions in the recipe.

In more precise terms, when a cell needs to build a protein that will accomplish a specific task, the portion of DNA in charge of production of that protein "unzips." Messenger RNA matches up with the unzipped portion and reads the instructions encoded in that section. The mRNA then copies the code, or transcript, and carries the information out of the nucleus and into the cell's cytoplasm. There it meets with a ribosome, which interprets the genetic instructions and builds the protein.

Proteins can allow a cell to metabolize nutrients, carry out different functions, or build tissue. A cell produces different protein transcripts during different stages of life. Scientists use transcriptomics to catalog and quantify RNA molecules, specifically the messenger RNA. By looking at all of these messages at the same time, scientists can get a snapshot of what an organism is up to on the cellular level.

Lenz and her team work with scientists to collect samples of preadult and adult female *Neocalanus flemingeri* in the Gulf of Alaska. The team extracts mRNA from the copepods and sends it out to be sequenced. The team receives back millions of short chunks of genetic information. They then use a computer program to match these short chunks to a reference sequence for this species of copepod. By looking at the gene "expression profile," or the number of genes of each type, the team can learn which messages are being relayed in the animal's cells. For example, the mRNA extracted just as a female is "waking up" likely relates to restarting its body functions and triggering egg production. Messages from a few weeks later might be associated with egg laying.

Lenz and her colleagues have examined the mRNA of female *Neocalanus flemingeri* from diapause to egg laying. They have discovered that it takes about seven and a half weeks for a female to go from waking up to laying eggs. They also learned that females keep immature sperm in their bodies for many months. Male hormones in the female's body allow the sperm to fully mature after the female wakes up.

The team compares the genetic expressions of one individual to others in the same group and individuals in one part of the ocean to

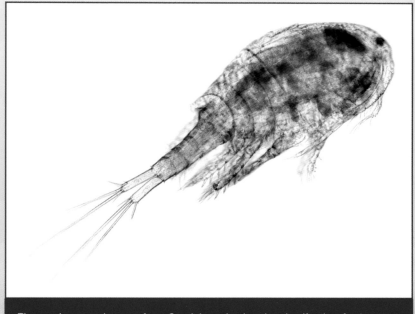

The word *copepod* comes from Greek kope (oar) and podos (foot), referring to the flat, oar-shaped swimming legs of these animals.

PROFILE: VITTORIA RONCALLI

POSTDOCTORAL RESEARCHER, UNIVERSITY OF BARCELONA, BARCELONA, SPAIN

Scientist Vittoria Roncali worked on Lenz's transcriptomics project. Roncalli studies zooplankton, which play "a key role in the energy transfer in the marine food web." She believes strongly in the importance of "understanding how zooplankton may respond to future climate scenarios— exploring the nature of their adaptive responses."

Since her work with Lenz, Roncalli has taken a postdoctoral research position at the University of Barcelona, where she is "investigating the effect of the toxic algae on the development of another zooplankter, the appendicular *Oikopleura dioica*." In all her work, she hopes to answer the questions, "How do organisms interact with/respond to their environment?" and "Why are organisms so successful in so many ecological niches in the aquatic environment?"

For students interested in careers in ocean sciences, Roncalli recommends pursuing "something that you are passionate about (yes, I was with copepods). Something that intrigues you. In addition to this, you want to work with someone who inspires and motivates you. When you find a mentor that opens your mind and helps you THINK out of the box, then all the rest comes easily. Maybe it is not so easy, but I wish [for] all of you, future scientists, to have my same good luck."

individuals in another part of the ocean. They can also use computer programs to connect the gene expressions of different groups of copepods to other data such as ocean temperature, acidity levels, and the type of phytoplankton present in the sample area. This helps scientists understand how these factors affect copepod physiology.

Lenz and her colleagues are continuing their work on how the life cycles of *Neocalanus flemingeri* respond to changing conditions. For instance, they've learned that these copepods can have a hard time building fat stores, which they need to survive dormancy and to complete egg laying. In locations and in years when their primary food consists of very small phytoplankton cells, the copepods are smaller and less robust, and they lay fewer eggs the next year.

Lenz and her team hope to create a reference tool to monitor populations of *Neocalanus flemingeri*. Then scientists can predict the abundance and quality of copepod populations prior to the fishing season, which will assist fisheries managers as they set catch limits. This will help Alaska's fisheries remain sustainable and marine food chains remain viable, even in the face of a changing climate.

CHAPTER 7

CITIES IN THE SEA

The sparkling waters of Kāne'ohe Bay off the island of Oahu hold a secret. Beneath the waves lies a bustling city. Fishes of all shapes, sizes, and colors weave and dart along alleys and streets. Garishly colored shrimp scuttle by, while slow-moving sea cucumbers take their time. Sea fans wave gently in the water, and a green sea turtle gracefully cruises overhead.

A closer look reveals tiny coral polyps, living creatures carpeting the city's actual structure. Coral polyps aren't just inhabitants—they are the architects and builders of the coral reef. Their importance to the ocean food web lies not in the food they provide to their predators but in the habitat they create for themselves and for every other creature that resides here.

Like many ocean animals, such as clams and mussels, coral polyps have the ability to manufacture calcium carbonate. Instead of shells that encircle them, coral polyps build structures beneath and around them. Most corals divide, creating identical daughter corals, which in turn grow and divide. Over time, these colonies build massive reefs, which lift the colony toward the sunlight. These reefs are full of nooks and crannies—prime real estate for other organisms. Stony coral scaffolding provides the perfect anchoring point for creatures such as sponges, anemones, and feather duster worms. Fishes, crabs, octopuses, eels, and many other species find safe hiding places. Sharks, turtles, rays, and sunfish visit the reef for a quick snack or for the cleaning services offered by parasite-gobbling fishes.

The habitats created by coral structures are the reason these ecosystems are among the most productive on Earth. Around the world, human communities rely directly on coral reefs for food. The reefs also provide shelter for the young of many commercially caught fishes, allowing them to survive to adulthood. And reefs draw tourists, further supporting local populations. The United Nations has estimated that coral reefs contribute hundreds of thousands of dollars per square kilometer to the world's economy each year. Moreover, coral reefs absorb wave energy, protecting coastal towns from high waves and storm surges. If coral reefs disappeared, some communities could experience waves as much as 2.4 times higher by 2100.

The Great Barrier Reef off the coast of Australia is the largest reef in the world, stretching for over 1,150 miles (1,850 km). Since 2016, over half the reef's coral has died from bleaching. Severe bleaching events used to occur in the region about every 27 years, but since the 1980s they have occurred every 6. The reef was struck two years in a row in 2016 and 2017, causing the massive die-off of coral. Reefs can take over a decade to rebound from such events.

A PARTNERSHIP IN PERIL

Reef-building (hard) corals partner with single-celled algae, called zooxanthellae, in a symbiotic relationship. Each polyp draws the algae into its inner tissue layer, where there can be millions of algae cells per square centimeter of coral tissue. Safe inside the polyp, the algae takes CO_2 and nutrients provided by the coral and energy provided by the sun to create sugars, which feed it and the coral polyp. This nutritional powerhouse provides the fuel the coral needs to build aragonite, the crystalline form of calcium carbonate that makes up the coral's skeleton.

This makes zooxanthellae critical to the health of coral reefs. Without them, reef-building coral polyps would struggle to find enough food and wouldn't be able to construct the structures they and so many other ocean creatures depend on. But the relationship is

DINNER WITH A SIDE OF ZOOPLANKTON

Reef-building corals rely on their partners—zooxanthellae—to provide them with a steady supply of food, but they also do a little "fishing" on the side. Like all cnidarians, including jellyfish and sea anemones, corals possess stinging cells called nematocysts. At night (for most species), each polyp unfurls a whorl of tentacles around a central mouth. When unsuspecting zooplankton swim into a tentacle, the toxins released by the nematocysts instantly immobilize them. The polyp then uses its tentacles to guide the food into its mouth. Though zooxanthellae provide much of the food a polyp requires, the zooplankton prey provide both the coral and its algae partners with important nutrients. The polyp gets an extra snack, and the zooxanthellae mines the waste products from the digested meal for nutrients it requires for photosynthesis.

A close-up view of the tentacles on a toadstool mushroom leather coral (*Sarcophyton sp.*). Corals use their tentacles to snag nutrients and particles out of the water.

tenuous. Under stress, corals will evict their algae partners. Stressors include extreme temperatures, pollution, excess UV radiation, or light levels that are too high or too low. Because coral tissue is somewhat transparent, coral without its algae partners appears white or "bleached." If conditions improve relatively quickly, coral can reestablish its partnership with the zooxanthellae and recover. Long-term stress, however, causes corals to die.

In 1996 and 2014, the reefs in Kāne'ohe Bay experienced bleaching. The bleaching event of 2014 to 2017 affected 75 percent of the world's coral reefs. Of these, 30 percent couldn't reestablish their partnerships with zooxanthellae and they died. Scientists are working to understand precisely why and how bleaching occurs to assess how much humans are impacting these ecosystems.

A NEW VIEW

Scientists examining the bleached corals in Kāne'ohe Bay noticed something intriguing. In some cases, patches of bleached coral were right next to patches of the same species of coral that had not expelled their zooxanthellae. One scientist in particular, Ruth Gates, wondered what was different about the coral that retained its algae partners. She and her research team set out to understand what makes some corals more resilient than others.

One major roadblock in their quest was that traditional light microscopes require scientists to create thin cross sections of tissue. Though this allows them to understand the structure of an organism, it doesn't let them see a living creature reacting to different stimuli. It doesn't allow them to see the polyps and their zooxanthellae interacting in their natural environment. And it doesn't let them see a polyp actually expelling its zooxanthellae. If all of these processes were to be observed, new technology was needed.

In 2011 the lab acquired a tool that allowed them to overcome some of these limitations—a laser scanning confocal microscope. The light source for this microscope is a laser, which illuminates the area of focus

OCEAN ACIDIFICATION AND CORAL REEFS

Ocean changes due to climate change impact corals in two ways. The first, warming temperatures, affect a coral's relationship with symbiotic zooxanthellae. The second, ocean acidification, interferes with a coral's reef-building ability. During reef building, corals extract carbonate from seawater and combine it with calcium and other chemicals to construct their calcium carbonate "skeletons." The coral creates these structures to get closer to the sunlight, so height is important. The coral also adds extra material to strengthen the skeleton so it is less vulnerable to breakage.

As the ocean absorbs more carbon dioxide, the water becomes more acidic, so less carbonate is available to corals and other shell- and structure-building ocean life. A study in 2018 by scientists from Woods Hole Oceanographic Institution pinpointed the impacts of ocean acidification on coral reefs. When less carbonate is available, corals appear to prioritize height over strength. This makes the reef structure more prone to damage from storms and currents, as well as from worms, crown-of-thorns starfish, and other sea life that bores through or preys on coral.

Coral bleaching events have occurred all over the world. This bleached finger coral (*Stylophora pistillata*) was photographed off the shore of Thailand.

PROFILE: EVA MAJEROVÀ

POSTDOCTORAL FELLOW, GATES LAB, UNIVERSITY OF HAWAI'I

Eva Majerovà, a scientist at the Gates Lab, works to "unveil the mechanisms some corals naturally acquire that make them more resilient to extreme weather events. Such knowledge would considerably help us to plan restoration strategies."

Majerovà began her career working in cancer research. She says, "During my first postdoctoral training in Brussels, Belgium, I focused on clinical research, studying processes that cancer cells use to become immortal. But my big passion for marine biology and the underwater world was constantly growing. I wanted to merge my biggest hobby with my professional career. I was very lucky because I met a brilliant and open-minded coral scientist, Ruth Gates, who was excited by the idea of applying clinical biology methods to the coral research. At the beginning of 2018, I joined her team at University of Hawai'i, where now I study bleaching and the death of corals on a molecular and cellular level."

Majerovà finds that the most compelling part of her work is "the feeling that I can help save one of the most beautiful and most important ecosystems on this planet. It is not always easy to be a scientist and to face all the obstacles the research for the unknown brings. But when I have a really hard day, I put my wet suit, mask, and fins on, swim to a coral reef, and watch the magnificent and peaceful underwater world. And then I know that every effort is worth fighting for its future."

more precisely than a traditional light microscope. A tiny pinhole makes sure that the detector only picks up light from the area that is illuminated by the laser, allowing for a much sharper image.

As the laser scans across the surface of the specimen, layer by layer, the detector gathers the light, pixel by pixel. The light is converted to digital information, which a computer uses to construct an image. This

INTO THE DEEP

allowed researchers, for the first time ever, to scan living pieces of coral rather than thinly sliced dead samples. Layer by layer, they viewed the organism in 3D and watched its activity change over time. There were a few surprises, such as when they discovered an unknown creature living with the coral. Though they aren't sure, Gates and her team think it might be a species of rotifer, a kind of zooplankton.

By subjecting samples of coral to different conditions and then viewing them under the laser scanning confocal microscope, Gates and the team at the Gates Lab confirmed that elevated water temperatures induce coral bleaching. The Gates Lab team continues to study the tissues of the coral and the zooxanthellae. They've used the microscope to examine the 3D structure of fragments of coral, rather than individual

SALUTE TO A CORAL CHAMPION

I have the upmost respect for corals. They're really sophisticated animals.

—Ruth Gates

Perhaps this is why Ruth Gates devoted much of her life to studying and saving these fascinating creatures. In her lab in Kāne'ohe Bay, Hawai'i, Gates focused on understanding what makes some corals more resilient during rising ocean temperatures and other stressors. Her groundbreaking work to breed "super corals" offers the hope that with a little help, coral reefs might be able to rebuild following devastating bleaching. Besides her scientific work, her steadfast belief that corals could be saved inspired many people.

Weeks after her death in October 2018, her team received a $1 million grant from the National Fish and Wildlife Foundation to attempt to restore reefs in Hawai'i with super corals. Kira Hughes, the lab's project manager, said that the team is "beyond excited, as this allows us to carry on Ruth's research vision. Most importantly, this allows lab members to stay together as a team, so we can carry out research in Ruth's honor."

polyps, to measure the density of zooxanthellae at the different locations. They are also studying the bleaching process to see if some zooxanthellae leave the coral on their own, rather than being expelled.

Other members of the lab use cutting-edge molecular biology and computer analysis to understand the molecular and cellular mechanisms underlying coral bleaching or affecting the corals' tolerance to heat stress. Team members also tend indoor and outdoor tanks that test corals' response to different temperatures and chemicals. The tanks also house efforts to breed corals that are more tolerant of warming conditions. Each data point collected helps scientists at the lab, and around the world, better understand the variables in bleaching. They are figuring out how and why some corals survive and others don't.

The race to save corals is on, and time may be running out. According to the January 11, 2019, issue of *Science* magazine, ocean warming is accelerating. That month the *New York Times* reported that one-fifth of corals have died over a three-year period. Charles Sheppard says in his work on corals that "reefs are more affected by the damaging consequences of climate change than any other known ecosystem." But a group of researchers in a small lab on an island in the Pacific Ocean refuses to give up. If corals continue to thrive in the oceans of the future, it may partly be thanks to the work of the late Ruth Gates and her team.

CHAPTER 8

FEEDING THE WORLD

Spring brings vast schools of silvery, spotted fish to the eastern Bering Sea. In open waters north of the Aleutian Islands, pollack have come to spawn. Each year, females lay up to two million eggs, which hatch in one to three weeks. Tiny larval fish join the plankton community, where they initially feed on phytoplankton. As they grow, copepods, krill, and other zooplankton make up the bulk of their diets. Adult pollack school near the ocean floor, where they feed on smaller fishes. Their speckled scales help hide them from predators lurking above.

The abundant availability of food in waters off the Alaska coast, combined with a high reproduction rate, has made the Alaskan coast the largest fishery in the United States. An average of 2.2 million tons (2 million t) of pollack are caught annually and go to the consumer market in many forms, including fast-food fish sandwiches, fish sticks, and imitation crab. Careful assessment of the population by scientists and fisheries managers ensures that enough fish remain to replenish the population in future years.

LEARNING TO REBUILD

Scientists and policy makers want to figure out the best way to harvest fish to feed the world while maintaining healthy fish populations and marine ecosystems. A combination of solutions, including catch limits set every year based on population levels, habitat protection, and no-fishing zones in spawning areas have helped some regions rebuild their fish stocks. The United States increased its percentage of sustainable fisheries from 53 percent in 2005 to 74 percent in 2016. Off the coast of Australia, 69 percent of fish stocks were fished at sustainable rates in 2015, up from 27 percent in 2004. And in the Northeast Atlantic, 60 percent of fish stocks are currently harvested sustainably, compared to 34 percent in 2003.

Off the western coast of the United States, populations of bottom fish species crashed in the late 1990s. Fishing operations struggled to make a living on smaller catches. The fishery was declared a federal

A fishing vessel brings in a haul off the coast of Alaska.

disaster in 2000, and strict new regulations went into effect. Huge swaths of ocean became off-limits to trawling, or bottom fishing. Fishing operations couldn't fish at all, not even for species that hadn't been affected by the crash. In open waters, rigid catch limits went into effect. Fishing operations lost their licenses, and many went out of business for good. For towns that depended upon commercial and recreational fishing, the regulations hurt, but the aim was to ultimately help the fisheries recover.

Fast-forward to the 2010s. Populations of all but three species made remarkable recoveries—decades sooner than scientists and fishery managers expected. In January 2019, catch restrictions were eased for many species, including perch, petrale sole, Pacific cod, and sablefish. The changes bode well for coastal communities, which could add hundreds of new jobs and tens of millions of dollars in increased income in 2019.

TRACKING FISH STOCKS

Establishing sustainable fisheries requires regular, accurate assessment of the number of fish in a given region. Scientists rely on several data sources to estimate fish stocks, including catch rates reported by fishing operations, annual population surveys conducted at sea, and biological information about sizes and ages of fishes caught within a particular area. The information is entered into a computer program, which projects future population levels, allowing fisheries managers to set better catch limits.

Fish population surveys are typically carried out with acoustic monitoring systems mounted on ships. This technology uses sound waves to detect large schools of fish. But ship time is expensive, and the amount of square miles a survey ship can cover on a voyage is limited. And ships can't survey fish stocks in shallow areas. To give scientists and fisheries managers a little help, NOAA scientists are testing unmanned saildrones.

TECH FOCUS: SAILDRONE

Saildrones have been deployed around the world to assist with a variety of ocean science missions. For example, they have plied the Southern Ocean on a quest to become the first autonomous vehicle to circumnavigate Antarctica. The first saildrone completed this trip on August 3, 2019. Saildrones have assisted researchers in the Gulf of Mexico and in the North Pacific. In 2019 they set sail in the North Sea to assist with studies on how fish group together.

Saildrones are autonomous vehicles that float on the ocean surface. They are outfitted with a sail for propulsion. Their wing tab design allows the vehicle to use minimal electric power to steer. Waypoints are sent to the vehicle's computer, which determines whether to tack or sail depending on wind conditions.

Instruments on the saildrones collect data about air and water temperatures, salinity, CO_2 levels, wave heights, and the presence of marine mammals. Though these vehicles are slower than ships, they have several advantages over large, expensive research vessels. They can operate year-round and can withstand rough seas. Solar panels power the equipment on the saildrones, which allows them to remain at sea for long periods without refueling. They can navigate shallow waters unreachable by ships, and operators can adjust the mission of a saildrone in real time.

The NOAA first began using saildrones in 2014, partnering with Saildrone to improve the vehicles' data collection abilities. Off the Alaska coast, NOAA researchers have used saildrones to gather information about ocean conditions, track endangered North Pacific right whales, survey walleye pollack populations, and track the prey of northern fur seals.

During the summer of 2018, researchers deployed and tested five saildrones off the western coast of North America. The test was a

HAKE: THE FISH YOU'VE PROBABLY EATEN BUT NEVER HEARD OF

Hake, also known as Pacific whiting, are a deep-water fish with mild white flesh similar to that of cod. An important link in the ocean food web, they feed on shrimp, krill, and smaller fish such as herring. Cod, rockfish, sharks, and marine mammals eat hake. The hake fishery is one of the most commercially important on the West Coast. Almost the whole fish is used in everything from fish sticks to fish oil supplements to animal feed. Surimi, a hake product, is also known as imitation crab and is often found in California sushi rolls.

The hake fishery uses a pelagic net, or mid-water trawl, which does not damage fragile ocean floor habitats. With these nets, the rate of bycatch—animals unintentionally caught—is very low. Protecting ocean habitats and avoiding bycatch are two of the criteria for a fishery to be considered sustainable.

partnership between Saildrone, NOAA, Cascadia Research Collective, and Fisheries and Oceans Canada. The saildrones included newly added acoustic technology designed to measure fish abundance. Scientists wanted to assess whether "autonomous data collection can improve the effectiveness and efficiency of fisheries management on the West Coast." During the test, four drones duplicated the route of NOAA Fisheries ship *Reuben Lasker*. Ship-based acoustics collected data on populations of sardines, anchovies, and other small fishes, while the saildrone also surveyed for hake. The fifth saildrone was used to try out different surveying methods to help scientists improve the efficiency and accuracy of stock assessments.

Scientists hoped to learn if data from the autonomous vehicles would be of high enough quality for fish stock surveys. They also needed to determine if the saildrones could keep up with the survey ships, enhancing the reach of the surveys rather than slowing the mission.

According to Larry Hufnagle, who led the hake surveys, the saildrones were responsive and robust. Together the five vehicles traveled more than 18,500 miles (29,773 km). The four saildrones attached to the NOAA research vessel collected similar data to see if adding saildrones

PROFILE: LARRY HUFNAGLE

ENVIRONMENTAL COMPLIANCE COORDINATOR AND ADVANCED TECHNOLOGIES DEVELOPMENT, NOAA NWFSC, SEATTLE, WASHINGTON

Larry Hufnagle was part of the NOAA's mission that tested saildrones off the western coast of the United States during the summer of 2018. Hufnagle studied biology and chemistry in college. He began his career in analytical chemistry and toxicology, but he says, "I found I liked field work too, so I moved to a division that conducted fisheries surveys. Since I had instrumentation experience, I moved to the then newly formed acoustics team, which is responsible for the biennial Pacific Hake Acoustic-Trawl Survey. My role was [to handle] survey gear, operations, logistics, and advanced technologies. From there I advanced to the Team Lead role and currently work at the Center level as the environmental compliance coordinator and in advanced technologies development."

Hufnagle enjoys "exploring, learning, and developing new methods using advanced technologies." He says that although there are many paths to a role like his, including studying biology, chemistry, or oceanography, "expertise in engineering and physics are also needed to bring advanced technologies and remote sampling techniques to fisheries research."

to ship surveys can improve data collection. The fifth saildrone continued its mission into 2019, testing its ability to navigate near-shore waters, and following migrating anchovies and other fishes. The months of testing helped scientists learn how to use the saildrone technology more efficiently to augment ship-based data collection.

The 2018 results were promising. Fish stock assessments affect the livelihoods of many people, so researchers want to ensure that new technology will enhance rather than disrupt data collection. If future tests are successful, saildrones may become a regular partner on NOAA survey missions, helping scientists and fisheries managers assess fish stocks to assure their health and viability.

Around the globe, fish stocks are in trouble. The double threat of climate change and overfishing may lead to population collapse in many areas. But it's not too late. Scientists and fisheries managers have shown that regular assessment of fish stocks and stringently enforced catch limits can restore balance to fish populations and reboot healthy fisheries. Researchers can harness high-tech tools such as saildrones to establish sustainable fisheries worldwide.

CHAPTER 9

RISE OF THE JELLYFISH

Jellyfish are mesmerizing animals. Their domed bells undulate rhythmically, propelling them slowly through the water. Delicate tentacles sway in the current, long and thin or ribbonlike and lacy. Their translucent bodies come in an astounding array of colors and patterns. The smallest species could fit on the tip of your pinkie finger. The largest have a bell about the size of a Smart car.

For all their grace and beauty, jellyfish can be dangerous. Their tentacles bear stinging nematocysts. Depending on the species and what or who the jellyfish brushes against, some can deliver venom that ranges from painful to deadly. In a single weekend in January 2019, about twenty-six hundred people in Queensland, Australia, received treatment for bluebottle jellyfish stings. And humans aren't the only victims. In Norway, for instance, swarms of jellyfish regularly invade salmon farms. Their stings injure the fish, making them more vulnerable to deadly bacteria, which leads to mass die-offs. Scottish fish farms have had similar issues. In 2014 a jellyfish invasion killed three hundred thousand young salmon.

Jellyfish swarms, or "blooms," also threaten coastal power plants. They use seawater to cool the machinery. Though filters prevent debris and animals from entering, they are no match for thousands of jiggling, gooey jellyfish, which can swiftly clog the waterways. Without adequate seawater flowing in, the plants are forced to shut down until the clog can be cleared. Jellyfish blooms closed down a coal-fired plant in Australia back in 1937, so this isn't a new problem. But each power plant closure costs millions of dollars in lost revenue.

Given their proclivity to suddenly rise in great masses seemingly out of nowhere, jellyfish have inspired doomsday predictions. When scientists openly wondered if warming waters might be contributing to increasing jellyfish populations, the headlines went wild. In 2013 ABC News declared, "Monsters of the Deep: Jellyfish Threaten the World's Seas." Other headlines screamed, "Jellyfish Are Taking Over the Seas, and It Might Be Too Late to Stop Them," and "The Jellyfish Are Coming: Brace Yourself for Goomageddon."

Armies of jellyfish make great news stories, but are there more of them than ever? Are jellyfish-clogged waters really a result of warming oceans or perhaps changes to pH levels? Or is the answer simply that overfished waters encourage the proliferation of food that jellyfish like to eat? When scientists started asking these questions about a decade ago, they realized they would need more data if they hoped to explain the "jellyfish explosion."

CHAPTER 10

LIFE IN THE TWILIGHT ZONE

While caves and reefs and even shipwrecks dot the seafloor, most of the ocean is open water. There are no physical features for life to live in and around. Another constant in most of the ocean is darkness. The sun begins to lose its intensity the instant it hits water. Only the first 656 feet (200 m) or so—the epipelagic zone—has enough light to support photosynthesis. From there to 3,280 feet (1,000 m)—the mesopelagic zone—sunlight decreases rapidly, barely casting a dim glow. By 3,280 feet, it disappears altogether.

Animals in this environment have developed unique adaptations to find food and avoid predators. One strategy of many species is to use the darker layers to hide from predators. A brilliant solution, except that the deep ocean lacks the abundant food resources of the sunlit zones. How do they hide from predators *and* get a good meal? Many species have solved this dilemma by taking a daily journey.

ZONES OF THE OCEAN

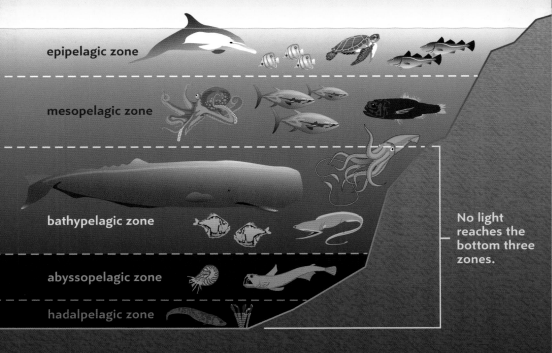

epipelagic zone

mesopelagic zone

bathypelagic zone

No light reaches the bottom three zones.

abyssopelagic zone

hadalpelagic zone

At sunset in the open ocean, the evening commute begins. Millions of tiny zooplankton rise from the dimly lit mesopelagic, or "twilight" zone, to feed nearer to the surface. Micronekton, organisms from 0.79 to 4 inches (2 to 10 cm) long, merge into the traffic, hoping for a nice meal of zooplankton. The micronekton—squid, small fishes, and shrimp, to name a few—attract larger fishes, including tuna, sharks, and swordfish. The game of eat and try not to be eaten stretches through the night. As sunrise approaches, those who have survived another night descend to dimmer waters with full bellies to await the next sunset.

TECHNOLOGY ON THE DEEPEND RESEARCH VESSELS

Scientists on the DEEPEND project use many kinds of technology during a research mission. Tracey Sutton describes a few tools used on the DEEPEND mission as follows: "First, we use nets to physically sample the deep sea. This is important because we still do not have a proper inventory of what lives in the deep. In order to understand this, we need to examine physical specimens. Second, to get a larger-scale view of the distribution of life throughout the water column, or across large stretches of ocean, both during the day and night, we use acoustic technology, similar to 'fish finders' anglers use, or radar that air-traffic controllers use. Lastly, to understand how different sections of the ocean control where things live, we look at the physical properties of water from satellites. This allows us to define 'water masses,' which act as different habitat types for animals that swim freely throughout the oceans."

Tracey Sutton oversees the deployment of MOCNESS during a DEEPEND expedition on the Gulf of Mexico.

INTO THE DEEP

PROFILE: NINA PRUZINSKY

RESEARCH ASSOCIATE AND LAB MANAGER, OCEANIC ECOLOGY LABORATORY, NOVA SOUTHEASTERN UNIVERSITY

In her research, Nina Pruzinsky focuses on poorly understood life stages, species, and communities in the ocean. She hopes to provide "information to the public and conservation/management efforts to help maintain populations and overall large ecosystems." This goal brought her to Tracey Sutton's Oceanic Ecology Laboratory and to the DEEPEND project.

During the DEEPEND project, Pruzinsky worked to develop "a synthesis of physical characteristics used to identify taxonomically challenging larval and juvenile life stages" of tuna. She also identified tuna present in DEEPEND's surveys. She says that "these cruises were amazing opportunities that enabled me to lead the data management/organization of the cruises, interact with numerous colleagues, have hands-on experience at sea, and work with fresh specimens. Seeing the striking colors (blues, reds, yellows) of the deep-sea organisms' barbels and photophores is truly incredible!"

INTO THE DEEP

Between 2015 and 2018, the research vessel *Point Sur* sailed into the Gulf of Mexico from Gulfport, Mississippi. On board were scientists from universities and institutions from across the United States. Their project, Deep Pelagic Nekton Dynamics Consortium (DEEPEND), sought to build a picture of the pelagic ecosystem of the northern Gulf of Mexico. By understanding the current condition of deep-water

TECH FOCUS: MOCNESS

A Multiple Opening and Closing Net and Environmental Sensing System, or MOCNESS, can be configured differently depending upon what is needed during an expedition. The DEEPEND team used a MOCNESS outfitted with six nets, sensors, and an echo sounder.

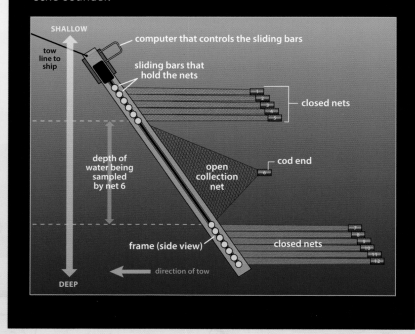

SHALLOW
tow line to ship
computer that controls the sliding bars
sliding bars that hold the nets
closed nets
depth of water being sampled by net 6
open collection net
cod end
frame (side view)
closed nets
direction of tow
DEEP

habitats and cataloging and studying the species there, they could establish a baseline to help future scientists detect natural and human-caused changes.

Over the course of five years, the team conducted twelve expeditions to study the creatures inhabiting the Gulf's open ocean and the relationship between these organisms and those in other ocean zones. To collect samples for study in the lab, they dropped different kinds of nets to various depths, from the surface to 2.8 miles (4.5 km).

Nina Pruzinsky examines elongated bristlemouth (*Sigmops elongatus*) specimens collected during a 2018 DEEPEND research cruise. Tissue samples collected from the fish were used for genetic barcoding and chemical analysis.

One net the scientists used is a sophisticated system called MOCNESS, or Multiple Opening and Closing Net and Environmental Sensing System. The frame of a MOCNESS can support six to twenty nets of varying mesh and opening sizes, depending on the needs of the researchers. The MOCNESS system used by DEEPEND featured six nets with a mesh size of 0.1 inches (3 mm). A conducting (wired) cable connects the frame to a winch system on the boat, which allows the net operator to open and close the nets while the system is underwater.

The MOCNESS net allows the team to collect samples from different depths and keep them separate from one another. Organisms caught by the net end up in the "cod end"—the container at the end of each net.

PROFILE: TRACEY SUTTON

ASSOCIATE PROFESSOR, NOVA SOUTHEASTERN UNIVERSITY AND DIRECTOR AND PRINCIPAL INVESTIGATOR, DEEPEND

Tracey Sutton first imagined life as a scientist at the age of six. He focused on marine studies in his middle school and high school classes as much as he could, and pursued his dream in college. After obtaining an MA and then a PhD in biological oceanography, he obtained a postdoctoral fellowship at the Woods Hole Oceanographic Institution, where he developed his research program in the deep sea. Since then he has worked on deep-sea projects in the North Atlantic, the Sargasso Sea, the Gulf of Mexico, and the Southern Ocean.

To students interested in pursuing marine science, Sutton advises "choosing a college that has an established marine science program, which will prepare you for graduate school. It is very important along the way to pay special attention to learning how to write well, as this seems to be a skill that is decreasing. No matter what we think we do as scientists, all we really do is write. If you do not write (publish) your research, you didn't really do it. Once in graduate school, it is important to pick a topic that REALLY appeals to you. Being a marine scientist will not make you rich financially, but is an extremely rewarding profession. It requires a LOT of hard work, and that generally happens when you love what you do."

The MOCNESS frame also supports sensors that measure depth, temperature, salinity, and water volume that passes through the net. This information is relayed to the boat in real time. It is recorded so researchers can match water conditions to the organisms found at each level. DEEPEND researchers have also attached a battery-powered echo sounder to the MOCNESS apparatus. Acoustic studies at the surface can detect where organisms are massed in the water. With echo sounders mounted to the MOCNESS, scientists can detect individual animals. This permits a much more precise estimate of how many animals are in a given area and allows researchers to observe behavior without turning on the lights.

Samples collected by the MOCNESS during DEEPEND's research missions were carefully recorded, cataloged, and preserved for further study. The samples collected have already revealed new species never before identified by science and species that had not previously been recorded in that region. Researchers will continue to use the samples in future studies. During the twelve DEEPEND expeditions, the MOCNESS deployed 122 times and spent 671 hours in the water. Scientist Heather Judkins reports that DEEPEND's trawls collected "61 cephalopod species, 120 crustacean species and 625 fish species! These are important numbers as in the past the midwater habitat was not considered a particularly diverse region."

The DEEPEND project, along with efforts like it worldwide, has helped reveal a little-known ocean zone. Researchers continue to deploy nets and other technology, such as remotely operated cameras and echo sounders, to discover more about the inhabitants of the mesopelagic and other deep-ocean layers. The more we learn, the more we find that no part of the ocean is without life. We also learn that no part of the ocean is removed from our lives here on land, and that efforts to understand strange and fantastic deep-water creatures are the first step to protecting them and ourselves.

CHAPTER 11

IN THE COMPANY OF GIANTS

The sea shelters the largest living creature on the planet. At about 90 feet (27 m) long and weighing up to 200 tons (181 t), a blue whale rivals the largest known dinosaurs. Its heart can grow up to the size and weight of a small car, and its vocalizations are among the loudest animal calls on Earth. Despite its tremendous size, the blue whale occupies an unlikely spot in the ocean food web. Rather than ruling the seas and fiercely dominating all smaller creatures, blue whales are filter feeders. To feed, they ingest massive mouthfuls of water and food. Where many other animals have teeth along the upper jaw, blue whales have a series of overlapping plates called baleen. The whale uses its tongue to push the water back out the mouth between the baleen plates. Its favorite food, small crustaceans called krill, get trapped. The largest blue whales can consume up to 6 tons (5.4 t) of krill per day.

The presence of these ocean giants affects the ocean food web in ways we have only just begun to understand. For example, baleen whales, the group that includes blue whales, play a role in the carbon cycle when they consume mouthfuls of krill and other small ocean life. Some of this carbon remains in the whale's body for a long time. Respiration and excretion expels the rest. Waste released as huge quantities of fluffy, floating poop fertilizes the ocean surface layer. These nutrients fuel phytoplankton growth, causing the removal of more carbon from the atmosphere, as well as supporting the ocean life that depends on these primary producers. Many baleen whales also migrate from rich, productive waters nearer the poles to areas nearer the equator, where whale poop is a boon to these nutrient-poor waters.

As we begin to understand more fully the influence that baleen whales have on their ecosystems, we've realized how profoundly the loss of these animals affects the entire planet. Before the nineteenth-century whaling industry nearly wiped out some of the larger whale species, the ocean sequestered more carbon that it does currently. A 2010 study estimated that before nineteenth-century whaling, the biomass of eight of the largest whale species exceeded 103 million tons (93 million t), and they removed around 192,700 tons (174,800 t) of carbon from the atmosphere every year. By contrast, biomass in 2001 was estimated at just under 16 million tons (15 million t), and whales were removing just under 29,000 tons (26,300 t) of carbon per year.

As a dead whale sinks to the bottom of the ocean, entire communities of organisms, from microbes to sharks, feed on its remains. Though the soft tissues disappear in a matter a months, a whale fall on the ocean floor may provide habitat and food for some benthic organisms for years.

Furthermore, whales' impact as nutrient cyclers and food sources would have supported a much more life-filled ocean. In a study released in 2014, scientist Joe Roman speculated that the "earliest human-caused extinctions in the sea may have been whale fall invertebrates, species that evolved and adapted to whale falls. . . . These species would have disappeared before we had a chance to discover them." *Whale fall* refers to a dead whale sinking and then coming to rest on the ocean floor, where organisms feed on the carcass.

WHEN FEAR BRINGS BALANCE

Though baleen whales and other filter feeders may not appear to be fierce hunters, they are considered apex predators because they eat other animals and have few predators themselves. But plenty of large ocean animals more closely resemble our image of an apex predator, including toothed whales, such as orcas and dolphins; most sharks; and large species of squid. The importance of these animals extends beyond teeth

INTO THE DEEP

and blood. Their presence in an ecosystem often has unexpected benefits.

For example, in Shark Bay in Western Australia, seagrass meadows stretch over 1 million acres (0.4 million ha), the largest expanse of this type of habitat in the world. Seagrass meadows are among the most productive ecosystems in the ocean. Young fishes shelter in the grass, avoiding hungry mouths that lurk above. Tiny snails and crustaceans feed on bacteria and algae that build up on the grass. Shellfish, worms, and anemones inhabit the sand substrate. These small inhabitants attract larger creatures. Large fishes and cephalopods—octopus, squid, and cuttlefish—prowl the clear, shallow water on the hunt for food. Green sea turtles graze on the abundant grass. The seagrass expanse is also home to 10 percent of the world's dugongs, a threatened marine mammal related to manatees.

Seagrass meadows benefit human populations as well. They shelter the young of important fish stocks, supporting industrial fisheries.

GENTLE GIANTS

The largest fish species, the whale shark, is also a filter feeder. Unlike their relatives, such as great white sharks and tiger sharks, whale sharks primarily feed on plankton, the eggs of marine animals, and small fishes. Seawater passes from mouth to gills, where food items are filtered out by gill rakers. Gill rakers in whale sharks act as a sieve, allowing water to pass through but trapping everything bigger than about 0.1 inches (2 to 3 mm). Whale sharks can grow longer than 40 feet (12 m) and weigh around 12 tons (11 t).

Whale sharks travel great distances to feed. Many visit coral reefs in Western Australia in March and April when most of the coral spawn on a single night. The waters of the Ningaloo Reef, already populated with plankton and small fishes, fill with millions of coral eggs. The whale sharks cruise through, mouths agape, feeding on the bounty.

PROFILE: LEIGH TORRES

ASSISTANT PROFESSOR, OREGON STATE UNIVERSITY, OREGON

Leigh Torres leads the Geospatial Ecology of Marine Megafuna Lab at the Marine Mammal Institute at Oregon State University. She studies whale behavior, ecology, and conservation. Through her research, she would like to learn how whales find food. Because "we cannot hold whales in captivity, it's very hard to figure the answer out just through observation."

The search for creative new ways to study whales led Torres and her team to try out drones. Drones offer the advantage of being "a non-invasive and relatively cheap and safe way to observe whale behavior, especially when we can see through the water and assess their body shape and condition."

During the summer, Torres's work takes her out to sea in a small boat regularly. She says, "We look [for] and find whales, and then we observe them from the boat and drone. We collect data on many aspects of their behavior, habitat, health, and prey. Then, when not in the field, we spend a lot of time in front of the computer analyzing these data and looking for patterns and trends."

Torres hopes her research helps us understand better "how whales respond to habitat change, from noise to climate change. How much can they withstand, and how do they adjust their behavior?"

a complete replacement for in-person and camera-based observations, eDNA analysis helps inform researchers which animals inhabit or pass through a particular habitat.

Like acoustic surveys for fish populations, eDNA testing can help scientists and resource management agencies determine the best places

Whales expel air, microbes, and fluids from their blowholes. To create SnotBot, engineers modified a drone to make it better able to withstand exposure to wind, sea spray, and, most important, whale snot.

to focus habitat preservation efforts. In time, eDNA analysis may help us improve our worldwide census of marine life and focus our efforts to protect ocean biodiversity.

Drone technology has also made monitoring large ocean species easier. Leigh Torres from Oregon State University uses drones outfitted with wildlife research–specific cameras to get a bird's-eye view of gray whales feeding off the Oregon coast during the summer and fall. Although about twenty thousand whales migrate past this region every year, about two hundred individuals remain in the area for weeks at a time.

Though scientists can spot whales from a research vessel, it's challenging to assess the condition of an individual from that angle. The whales can only really be seen when they surface. Because drones fly far above the ocean's surface, Torres can see an animal from above and assess its approximate length and girth. This allows her to calculate the individual's body adiposity (fat) index (BAI). BAI is similar to body mass index (BMI) in humans and can be an indicator of an animal's health. In whales, fat allows for energy storage and therefore thinner animals— those with smaller BAIs—may be malnourished. Torres also collects and analyses fecal samples, from which she can measure stress levels. Gray whales can be stressed by marine noise pollution, boat traffic, and other ocean conditions. By combining data gathered by the drones with the fecal sample analysis, Torres can more easily track the health of individual whales over time.

Working with Ocean Alliance, scientists from Olin College have also enlisted the drones for help. They fly modified drones they've dubbed SnotBots to about 12 feet (3.6 m) above a whale and through its "blow," or exhalation, collecting samples of whale mucous. The samples teem with microbes such as viruses and bacteria. They hope to use these samples to assess the microbial communities in different populations of whales. As they more fully understand these communities, they'll be able to assess when an animal is sick. The samples also contain DNA and hormones that can indicate if an animal is stressed or even pregnant. Initial testing of the SnotBots successfully collected 171 samples from five whale species. Next, researchers and engineers will work to improve and further test the technology.

While rebuilding whale populations alone will not solve the climate crisis our planet faces, it would have a substantial effect. Predators too play an essential role in the health of oceans. Restored to their rightful places in ocean ecosystems, they bring balance to populations of organisms lower down in the food web competing for resources. Armed with determination and a few well-chosen tools, researchers continue to work to understand these awe-inspiring, life-giving animals. They hope this knowledge will lead policy makers around the globe to create further protections for these species.

INTO THE DEEP

CHAPTER 12

WASTE NOT, WANT NOT

When a hunt in the ocean or on land ends in success for the predator, there are often leftovers. These bits, along with cells, skin, scales, feathers, and poop left behind by every living thing in the water, are collectively called detritus. Detritus is food for the "recycling team" in the food web, officially known as detritivores.

Detritus is immediately colonized by ravenous microbes, which form entire communities around the particles. Near the surface, copepods and other zooplankton catch bits of detritus and eat them. In turn, waste from these tiny creatures becomes part of the sinking feast. Some particles stick together as they sink, forming loose clumps oceanographers call "marine snow."

Farther down, some of the particles might pass a mucous structure built by a larvacean. Larvaceans are gelatinous zooplankton that range from 0.08 to 3.9 inches (0.2 to 10 cm), depending on the species. They construct mucous "nets" many times bigger than themselves and pump their tails to generate currents so particles pass through the nets. The outer walls of the slimy structures capture particles too large for the larvacean to eat. Smaller particles pass into the inner structure. The larvacean also uses currents generated by its tail to move food particles into its mouth. Several times a day, the "house" becomes clogged with particles. When this happens, the larvacean abandons the old house and creates a new one.

The old tent joins the slow procession of decaying material. Flitting copepods mob these discarded houses, nibbling on them. The colony of microbes grows ever larger. As the particles keep sinking, fishes and crustaceans grab a quick snack. Bits from leftover feasts, along with poop, join the collection of sinking particles. Farther down, the detritus might be food for a vampire squid. Despite their fierce name, these squid have very different feeding habits than other cephalopods. Vampire squid extend two long filaments into the water column. Bits of marine snow stick to the filaments, and then the squid retracts the filaments and eats the bits.

All the way down, the remnants of a feast at the ocean surface feeds ocean life. Weeks later, the remaining particles reach the ocean floor. Very few arrive in their original state. Most of the material that started as the leftovers at the surface has been broken down by microbes, eaten, pooped out, eaten again, and broken down by microbes again—or recycled several times over. Still, whether the material arrives in its original condition or as recycled goods, marine snow is the primary food source for the deep-ocean and benthic ecosystems. Worms, sea cucumbers, urchins, and some species of fish rely on this source of food. They are then eaten by other benthic and demersal (near the ocean floor) organisms. Scientists think that about 1 percent of the 16 gigatons (18 billion tons, or 16 billion t) of carbon initially produced per year by phytoplankton at the ocean surface eventually makes its way to the seafloor, though it has usually been eaten and "repackaged" several times before it does. Though the overall percentage seems small, 1 percent is just over 150 million tons (136 million t) per year—enough to sustain diverse communities both on the seafloor and in the sediments.

INTO THE DEEP

PROFILE: MAUREEN H. CONTE

ASSOCIATE SCIENTIST, BERMUDA INSTITUTE OF OCEAN SCIENCE, BERMUDA, AND FELLOW, MARINE BIOLOGICAL LABORATORY, MASSACHUSETTS

Maureen Conte describes the ocean as a "three-dimensional world that houses the largest ecosystems on earth. The ocean sustains life on earth. We couldn't survive without the oxygen that the ocean phytoplankton produces, not even if we live in the middle of the continent! And not even the deep ocean is immune to climate disruption."

The focus of Conte's work is to "understand the processes that control the movement of energy and materials through the ocean, from the surface to the seafloor."

Conte describes her time at sea during research missions as "long and tiring," but also "exciting." She says, "The work dictates when I get up, and when I might get a chance for a nap. I'm always conscious of the sky, the wind, and the weather, and have to struggle with modifying work plans when seas get rough. Generally I spend a lot of my day either out on the stern of the ship (the fantail) deploying equipment to collect water or particle samples, or in the ship's lab processing the samples I've collected. Often I'm out of the deck with our team recovering the mooring—which is a grueling day—and afterwards preparing the instruments for redeployment. The next day we're again back out of the deck deploying the mooring. I like that the instruments on the mooring will keep busy sampling the ocean until we're back again at the site in six months' time. Meal times are really important breaks to keep fueled, but also to relax and just hang for a spell with other scientists and crew members sharing stories and adventures. We all come from such different backgrounds!"

Maureen Conte and her team retrieve a sediment trap from the Sargasso Sea in the Atlantic Ocean. The white sample collection bottles on the sediment trap carousel can be clearly seen at the base of the yellow trap funnel. A fresh bottle rotates into position under the trap funnel every two weeks. The days when the team extracts the traps are the most grueling.

material is then freeze-dried and analyzed chemically. About 30 percent of the material is preserved in a solvent so scientists can analyze its molecular composition. The final amount of the sample is freeze-dried for later analysis of its elemental composition.

Evaluation of each sample over more than forty years has shown that the availability of food in the deep ocean is related to the seasonal cycle of phytoplankton blooms at the surface, as well as to long-term changes in surface ocean conditions and climate patterns. For example, in the spring of 2007, a pattern of ocean eddies increased the availability of nutrients at just the right time for the spring phytoplankton bloom. This triggered a bloom much larger than normal. The massive bloom led

INTO THE DEEP

PROFILE: J. C. WEBER

SENIOR RESEARCH ASSISTANT, MARINE BIOLOGICAL LABORATORY, MASSACHUSETTS

J. C. Weber has worked on the Oceanic Flux Program for twenty-three years and uses a variety of technology. "We use microscopes and digital cameras to see the diverse contents of the samples we collect with our sediment traps. It still amazes me how [much] the composition can vary between the two-week samples, reacting to changes in the season or [to] brief but impactful events like storms or oceanographic eddies. The deep sea is a wondrous place and after all of this time, I still see things I've never seen along with the beautiful usual shells and particles.

"We also use a variety of elemental analyzers to look at the chemical composition of the particles learning information about their source and changes over time. We use a Gas Chromatograph Mass Spectrometer to identify and quantify the organic chemical biomarkers that we extract from the particles in the sample adding more resolution to information about the particle sources and the processes they have encountered as they sink and transform. We can even look at the stable isotopes in the carbon and nitrogen of these particles and biomarkers to gain even more insight."

Weber advises that students interested in pursuing marine science think about which aspects of this discipline interest them. He says, "Explore online, look at the project websites for information on the work of specific groups and don't be shy to reach out with an email or letter for more information. When choosing courses in college, it is very important to build a strong multidisciplinary foundation in sciences. There's plenty of time to specialize in graduate school or with experience on the job."

Rut Pedrosa Pàmies and J. C. Weber examine samples collected by the Oceanic Flux Program's sediment traps. Although seafloor sediments form from only a tiny fraction of the material that survives transit through the water column, they retain a wealth of physical and chemical signatures of the overlying ocean conditions which are used by scientists to reconstruct past ocean and climate history.

to a huge increase in the flow of phytoplankton detritus, which fueled an increase in zooplankton grazing activity, and in the production of waste and other debris discarded by organisms feeding on the sinking particles. The increased phytoplankton production at the surface meant more food for deep-ocean animals as well. Conversely, during periods of low phytoplankton production, the particle flux in the deep ocean is lower.

Scientists working on the Oceanic Flux Program have also discovered evidence that links the deep-ocean particle flux to a large-scale weather pattern—the North Atlantic Oscillation. It measures

INTO THE DEEP

the pressure difference between Iceland, which typically has lower atmospheric pressure, and the Azores (a region of Portugal), which usually has higher atmospheric pressure. When the pressure differences between the two are less, the island of Bermuda typically experiences more winter storms and colder temperatures. These storms bring nutrients to the surface, which fuels larger phytoplankton blooms. Oceanic Flux Program researchers have discovered that during these years, the particle flux in the deep ocean is also higher. Though more research is needed over a longer period to confirm the details, probably changes in weather patterns due to climate change will affect life far below the surface. Data collected by the Oceanic Flux Program provide further evidence that every inch of the planet, from the deepest ocean depths to the peaks of mountains, is connected to every other inch, and the impact of climate change will touch every ecosystem.

CONCLUSION
OCEAN PAST, OCEAN FUTURE

E arth is a water world. No matter how far removed we are from its crashing waves, cool spray, and mysterious inhabitants, the ocean reaches us one way or another, perhaps through the weather we experience, the water we drink, or the seafood on our plates. More important, the ocean is a buffer between humans and our own worst enemy: ourselves. Without its role as temperature moderator and carbon sink, the planet's temperatures would be rising much more rapidly. Even with this buffering effect, climate change is creating profound consequences for the ocean, consequences that ultimately will impact human societies around the globe.

Will it really be that bad? Skeptics' voices have sounded ever since climate change emerged as a serious policy issue in the late 1970s. They gained strength over the next decade, and grew into a powerful disinformation campaign in the 1990s. As the effects of climate change progressed from prediction to reality, outright denial gave way to an insistence that warming temperatures and melting ice sheets are a natural phenomenon. Earth has warmed before. Who's to say this isn't just a normal part of Earth's climate cycle?

OCEAN PAST

To place current climate changes in context, we need to understand how Earth's climate has changed over time. Reliable records of conditions such as temperature and currents have only existed for about 150 years. Fortunately, the ocean has preserved a library of its past conditions. When detritus makes its way to the ocean floor, the portion that remains uneaten builds up, layer after layer. Also part of these growing layers are tiny bits of rocks and minerals. As time passes, the oldest layers are buried deeper and deeper. In this way, a library-like record of the past builds up over time. Scientists "check out" a volume of Earth's history by drilling into the ocean floor. Long tubes encase a sample of ocean sediment. One by one, these tubes are extracted and quickly brought to refrigerated facilities to protect the integrity of the samples. Depths of the samples are carefully recorded.

What can old dirt, ancient poop, and long-dead sea animals tell us about climate? Scientists rely on proxies, or indirect measurements, to determine probable conditions during a particular period. For example, different kinds of plankton and benthic species prefer different conditions. By assessing which species are present at a specific depth on a core sample, scientists can estimate ocean temperature, ice sheet distribution, and the productivity of the ocean during that period.

A more complex proxy can be found in chemical properties in the shells of fossilized foraminifera buried in ocean sediments. These common,

COMPUTING THE OCEAN

To assess what the future holds for the ocean, scientists turn to computer models. These models are built upon a handful of ocean physics equations. They describe properties such as water's momentum in three dimensions and the transport of heat and salt throughout the ocean. Some very simplified versions of these equations can be done by hand to give a big-picture view of how the ocean works. In reality, the system is much more complex. Water's movement in one small part of the ocean, combined with its temperature and salinity, affects the sections of ocean next to it, which interact with the sections next to them, and so on. Suddenly millions of equations are required to describe the interactions, and doing the work by hand is impossible.

To address these complexities, engineers write computer programs that divide the ocean into "boxes" or units that are 50 by 50 miles (80 by 80 km) at the surface, with a depth of anywhere from a foot to thousands of feet. Each box simulates the ocean's behavior based on the physics equations built into the program. Each box interacts with the boxes around it, and all the boxes together create a model that simulates how the global ocean works.

To project the future ocean, scientists input starting conditions such as temperature and salinity. They also specify boundary conditions, or conditions along the border between the ocean and other systems such as the atmosphere. Once these parameters are in place, no further input is required—the model starts chugging along. Thanks to the equations that describe ocean physics, the computer model can mimic the real thing, calculating the evolution of the ocean's properties years into the future.

To build a model that shows how the ocean affects and is affected by other components of Earth's climate, researchers build a model for each—ocean, land, ice, and atmosphere. A portion of the computer program, called a coupler, tells the models of each component what is happening within each of the other components. Changes to one

PROJECTIONS VS. PREDICTIONS

Climate models offer projections, a possible set of future conditions based on known ocean and atmospheric physics and current conditions. This differs from a prediction such as those we get from a meteorologist about this week's weather. When meteorologists use models, they continually update them based on real-time, changing conditions. This constant tweaking allows greater accuracy as the timeline grows shorter. This is why a forecast for the next twenty-four hours is more accurate than one for the next five days.

But computer climate models project future climate conditions based on an initial data set. While this data set can be continually updated and improved with new information, the level of precision is not the same as a meteorological model.

This doesn't invalidate the value of a climate model—the two have different purposes. A precise weather report helps school officials decide whether to close school the next day, while a climate model informs world leaders and policy makers trying to plan their approach to global climate change.

result in the appropriate changes to the others. For example, changes to surface wind patterns in the atmospheric model would result in surface current changes in the ocean model. In this way, scientists can project the ocean's influence on the other elements of the climate system and vice versa.

Because these models help policy makers and the public understand potential future ocean conditions, scientists are constantly working to improve the models' precision. Some improvements come with more advanced mathematical algorithms, which solve the equations more accurately. Additional computer power allows the "box" size to be reduced. Another way to improve the models is to acquire more data. The more we learn about the ocean from scientists around the world, the more precise the initial conditions entered into the computer model. Improved data also helps scientists refine initial models—adding aspects of ocean phenomena that had previously been undiscovered or poorly understood.

SAVING THE OCEAN AND THE PLANET

In April 2019, *Science* reported that the most up-to-date computer models project a more rapid rise in average temperature—up to 9°F

(5°C) before things balance out. This exceeds the previous projections by 3.6°F to 8.1°F (2°C to 4.5°C). News coming from every oceanography discipline is similarly urgent. Without intervention on our part, the ocean will continue to warm and grow more acidic, changing global weather patterns and becoming increasingly inhospitable for many ocean organisms.

Science illuminates the ocean. It reveals its physical and chemical properties and examines strange and wonderful creatures that call it home. It helps us understand how and why the sea affects our lives. But science cannot save it. Regulations and policies that can protect the ocean come from local, regional, and national governments and through international cooperation. And these entities are more likely to act when enough everyday people demand it. Our lives are bound to the ocean's fate, and our decisions will ultimately decide which computer projection becomes reality.

GLOSSARY

accelerometer: an instrument that measures motion and velocity

aquifer: an underground layer of permeable rock, sand, or gravel that holds water

bathymetry: the depth and shape of the seafloor

bathypelagic: the dark ocean depths between about 3,000 and 10,000 feet (1,000 to 3,000 m)

benthic: having to do with or living on the bottom of a body of water

cilia: tiny, hairlike projections

demersal: having to do with or living near the bottom of a body of water

deoxyribonucleic acid (DNA): a material in each cell that is self-replicating and carries an organism's genetic information

detritus: waste or debris

diapause: suspended development often employed by invertebrates to survive harsh conditions

diel vertical migration: the twice-daily movement of ocean organisms from the mesopelagic zone to the surface and back again

eukaryote: a life-form whose cells have nuclei

gigaton: one billion metric tons

hypoxia: the condition of low or depleted oxygen

interferometer: an instrument that merges two or more light or sound waves and measures the resulting interference patterns

intertidal: part of the seashore zone that is above water during low tide and below water during high tide

mesopelagic: the "twilight zone," a layer of ocean between 656 and 3,280 feet (200 to 1,000 m) where light gives way to darkness

microbes: small, single-celled life-forms that can only be seen with a microscope, including bacteria, algae, and fungi

micron: one millionth of a meter

multibeam echo sounder: a sonar device that sends multiple acoustic signals or "pings" to cover a wide swath of terrain

nematocysts: the stinging cells found in cnidarians, such as corals, jellyfish, and anemones

neutrally buoyant: neither more nor less buoyant

nucleus: the central part or core

ocean acidification: the decrease in ocean pH

ocean gyre: a large, circular system of ocean currents driven by a combination of wind patterns and Earth's rotation

oceanography: the study of the physical properties of the ocean and the organisms that live in it

organelle: a specialized structure within a living cell

pelagic: having to do with the open ocean

physiological: related to an organism's healthy or normal functioning

prokaryote: a single-celled organism that does not have a nucleus or specialized organelles

proxy: a record of physical conditions that can be used to estimate past climate conditions

thermohaline circulation: large-scale ocean circulation driven by differences in density

transcriptomics: the study of RNA transcripts, or genetic messages, produced by a cell

upwelling: an upward current in the ocean that brings cold, usually nutrient-rich water to the surface

zooxanthellae: symbiotic species of algae that live inside coral polyps

SOURCE NOTES

13 "How Much of the Ocean Have We Explored?" National Oceanic and Atmospheric Administration, https://oceanservice.noaa.gov/facts/exploration .html.

14 Megan Scanderbeg, email message to the author, June 3, 2019.

14 Scanderbeg.

19 "The Water Cycle: The Oceans," USGS Water Science School, last modified December 2, 2016, https://water.usgs.gov/edu/watercycleoceans.html.

23 "People," NASA, accessed February 6, 2019, https://gracefo.jpl.nasa.gov/about /people/.

34 Emery Nolasco, email message to the author, June 13, 2019.

34 Nolasco.

34 Nolasco.

41 Eleanor Frajka-Williams, "RAPID: Monitoring the Meridional Overturning Circulation at 26°N," Ocean Challenge 18 (Summer 2011), 16.

42 Eleanor Frajka-Williams, email message to the author, February 25, 2019.

42 Frajka-Williams.

42 Frajka-Williams.

50 Jonathan Peter Fram, email message to the author, May 23, 2019.

50 Fram.

50 Fram.

51 Mark Floyd, "Marine Ecologist Awarded NOAA Grant to Study Hypoxia in the Pacific Ocean," *iMPACT: Transformational Experiences in the College of Science*, Oregon State University, October 4, 2018, http://impact.oregonstate.edu /2018/10/marine-ecologist-awarded-noaa-grant-to-study-hypoxia-in-the-pacific -ocean/.

65 Flora Vincent, email message to the author, June 8, 2019.

65 Vincent.

69 J. Mauchline, *Advances in Marine Biology: The Biology of Calanoid Copepods* (San Diego: Academic, 1998), 1.

74 Vittoria Roncalli, email message to the author, February 17, 2019.

74 Roncalli.

74 Roncalli.

82 Eva Majerovà, email message to the author, February 26, 2019.

82 Majerovà.

82 Majerovà.

83 Ruth Gates, quoted in *Chasing Coral*, directed by Jeff Orlowski, produced by Larissa Rhodes, Exposure Labs, accessed July 14, 2017, https://www.chasingcoral.com.

83 Marcie Grabowski, "$1M Grant Boosts Coral Reef Restoration in Hawai'i, Expands Gates Coral Lab Research," *University of Hawai'i News*, University of Hawai'i, November 19, 2018, https://www.hawaii.edu/news/2018/11/19/grant-boosts-coral-reef-restoration/.

84 Charles Sheppard, *Coral Reefs: A Very Short Introduction* (Oxford: Oxford University Press, 2014), 98.

87 "Fish Stock Assessment 101," NOAA Fisheries, accessed February 19, 2019, https://www.st.nmfs.noaa.gov/Assets/stock/documents/Fish_Stock_Assessment_101.pdf.

87 *The State of World Fisheries and Aquaculture*, Food and Agriculture Organization of the United Nations (Rome: FAOUN, 2018), 6, http://www.fao.org/3/i9540en/I9540EN.pdf.

91 Michael Milstein, "Saildrones Join NOAA's West Coast Fleet for Experimental Fisheries Surveys," Northwest Fisheries Science Center, NOAA Fisheries, June 2018, https://www.nwfsc.noaa.gov/news/features/saildrone/index.cfm.

92 Lawrence Hufnagle, email message to the author, May 21, 2019.

92 Hufnagle.

95 Samiha Shafy and Spiegel, "Monsters of the Deep: Jellyfish Threaten the World's Seas," ABC News, July 13, 2013, https://abcnews.go.com/International/monsters-deep-jellyfish-threaten-worlds-seas/story?id=19647213.

95 Gwynn Guilford, "Jellyfish are Taking Over the Seas, and It Might Be too Late to Stop Them," *Quartz*, October 15, 2013, https://qz.com/133251/jellyfish-are-taking-over-the-seas-and-it-might-be-too-late-to-stop-them/.

95 Tamar Stelling, "The Jellyfish are Coming: Brace Yourself for Goomageddon," *Correspondent*, August 4, 2016, https://thecorrespondent.com/4831/the-jellyfish-are-coming-brace-yourself-for-goomageddon/.

97 Maria Temming, "New Robot Gently Grabs Sea Critters," *Science News Magazine* 194, no. 4 (August 18/September 1, 2018), 10.

97 "Norway Lobsters' Appetite for Jellyfish Caught on Camera," Phys.org, January 4, 2018, https://phys.org/news/2018-01-norway-lobsters-appetite-jellyfish-caught.html.

99 Kim Martini , email message to the author, June 17, 2019.

99 Martini.

99 Martini.

111 Heather Judkins, "As the MOC Comes Up," DEEPEND (blog), August 2, 2018, http://deependconsortium.org/index.php/blog/adults-blog/entry/as-the-moc -comes-up-heather-judkins/.

106 Tracey Sutton, email message to the author, February 25, 2019.

110 Sutton.

107 Nina Pruzinsky, email message to the author, March 1, 2019.

107 Pruzinsky.

114 Joe Roman, quoted in "Whales as Ecosystem Engineers," Phys.org, July 3, 2014, https://phys.org/news/2014-07-whales-ecosystem.html.

118 Leigh Torres, email message to the author, June 14, 2019.

118 Torres.

118 Torres.

118 Torres.

121 Emily Frost, "Marine Snow: A Staple of the Deep," Ocean: Find Your Blue, Smithsonian, January 2013, https://ocean.si.edu/ecosystems/deep-sea/marine -snow-staple-deep/.

123 Maureen H. Conte, email message to the author, June 14, 2019.

123 Conte.

123 Conte.

125 Rut Pedrosa Pàmies, email message to the author, June 16, 2019.

125 Pàmies.

127 J. C. Weber, email message to the author, June 14, 2019.

127 Weber.

132 "Ice Cores and Climate Change," British Antarctic Survey, March 1, 2014, https://www.bas.ac.uk/data/our-data/publication/ice-cores-and-climate -change/.

136 Andrew Shao, email message to author, June 13, 2019.

136 Shao.

136 Shao.

SELECTED BIBLIOGRAPHY

Anderson, Ross, and Christine Porr. "'Diese Flasche Wurde Uber Bord Geworfen': A Message in a Bottle from the German Barque *Paula* (1886) Discovered at Wedge Island, Western Australia." Report No. 325. Department of Maritime Archaeology, Western Australia Museum, February 2018. http://museum.wa.gov.au /maritime-archaeology-db/sites/default/files/ma_report_325_paula_bottle _message_020318_0.pdf.

"Autonomous Systems." Center for Coastal and Ocean Mapping Joint Hydrographic Center, University of New Hampshire, NOAA. Accessed February 7, 2019. http:// ccom.unh.edu/theme/autonomous-systems/.

Barth, Jack. "Winds, Coastal Circulation, Climate Variability, and Hypoxia off the Pacific Northwest." PowerPoint slides at Marine Ecosystems and Climate: Modeling and Analysis of Observed Variability, NCAR, Boulder, CO, August 5, 2009. http://www.cgd.ucar.edu/events/marine/presentations/Barth.2.pdf.

"Basics of Confocal Laser Scanning Microscopy." YouTube video, 35:41. Posted by ESRIC Microscopy, October 29, 2014. https://www.youtube.com/watch ?v=Nh4CnVZ9x8o.

"Benefits of Coral Reefs." United Nations, International Coral Reef Initiative (ICRI). Accessed February 14, 2019. https://www.icriforum.org/about-coral-reefs /benefits-coral-reefs/.

Boussarie, Germain, Judith Bakker, Owen S. Wangensteen, Stefano Mariani, Lucas Bonnin, Jean-Baptiste Juhel, Jeremy J. Kiszka, Michel Kulbicki, Stephanie Manel, William D. Robbins, Laurent Vigliola, and David Mouillot. "Environmental DNA Illuminates the Dark Diversity of Sharks." *Science Advances* 4, no. 5 (May 2018). http://advances.sciencemag.org/content/4/5/eaap9661.full.

Brierley, Andrew S. "Diel Vertical Migration." *Current Biology* 24, no. 22 (November 17, 2014). https://www.cell.com/current-biology/pdf/S0960-9822(14)01067-7.pdf.

Brusca, Richard C., and Gary J. Brusca. *Invertebrates*. Sunderland, MA: Sinauer, 2003.

Burkholder, Darek A., Michael R. Heithaus, James W. Fourqurean, Aaron Wirsing, and Lawrence M. Dill. "Patterns of Top-Down Control in a Seagrass Ecosystem: Could a Roving Apex Predator Induce a Behaviour-Mediated Trophic Cascade?" *Journal of Animal Ecology* 82, (2013). https://besjournals.onlinelibrary.wiley.com/doi/epdf /10.1111/1365-2656.12097.

Clancy, Suzanne, and William Brown. "Translation: DNA to mRNA to Protein." *Nature Education* 1, no. 1 (2008). https://www.nature.com/scitable/topicpage/translation -dna-to-mrna-to-protein-393.

Conte, M. H., and J. C. Weber. "Particle Flux in the Deep Sargasso Sea: The 35-Year Oceanic Flux Program Time Series." *Oceanography* 27, no. 1 (March 2014). http:// tos.org/oceanography/assets/docs/27-1_conte.pdf.

Cortissoz, Ann. "What's Next for SnotBot?" Ocean Alliance. Accessed February 25, 2019. https://whale.org/whats-next-for-snotbot/.

"DEEPEND: Deep Pelagic Nekton Dynamics of the Gulf of Mexico." DEEPEND. Accessed February 12, 2019. http://www.deependconsortium.org/.

Ebbesmeyer, Curtis C. "Beachcombing Science from Bath Toys." *Beachcombers' Alert*. Accessed February 8, 2019. http://beachcombersalert.org/RubberDuckies .html.

"FlowCam® for Phytoplankton & Zooplankton Analysis." Fluid Imaging Technologies. Accessed February 17, 2019. https://www.fluidimaging.com/applications /phytoplankton-and-zooplankton-analysis/.

Foden-Vencil, Kristian. "Coastal Pacific Oxygen Levels Now Plummet Once a Year." *Weekend Edition Saturday, NPR*, October 28, 2018. https://www.npr.org/2018 /10/28/658953894/coastal-pacific-oxygen-levels-now-plummet-once-a-year/.

Fossette, Sabrina, Kakani Katija, Jeremy A. Goldbogen, Steven Bograd, Wyatt Patry, Michael J. Howard, Thomas Knowles, Steven H. D. Haddock, Loryn Bedell, Elliott L. Hazen, Bruce H. Robison, T. Aran Mooney, K. Alex Shorter, Thomas Bastian, and Adrian C. Gleiss. "How to Tag a Jellyfish? A Methodological Review and Guidelines to Successful Jellyfish Tagging." *Journal of Plankton Research* 38, no. 6 (November 25, 2016). https://academic.oup.com/plankt /article/38/6/1347/2304825.

Frajka-Williams, Eleanor. "RAPID: Monitoring the Meridional Overturning Circulation at 26°N." *Ocean Challenge*, vol. 18 (Summer 2011), pp. 14–18. https://www .researchgate.net/publication/266190160_RAPID_Monitoring_the_meridional _overturning_circulation_at_26N/.

"GRACE-FO: Gravity Recovery and Climate Experiment Follow-On." Jet Propulson Laboratory. NASA. Accessed February 5, 2019. https://www.jpl.nasa.gov/news /brochure/gracefo_brochure.pdf.

"GRACE-FO Launch Press Kit." Jet Propulsion Laboratory, NASA, May 2018. https:// www.jpl.nasa.gov/news/press_kits/grace-fo/download/grace-fo_launch_press _kit.pdf.

"Landmark West Coast Survey Assesses Fish Stocks, Counts Marine Mammals, and Collaborates with Saildrone to Test New Technologies." Southwest Fisheries Science Center, NOAA, November 14, 2018. https://swfsc.noaa.gov/news.aspx ?ParentMenuId=287&id=23171.

Learn, Joshua Rapp. "The Upside of Rising Jellyfish Numbers? Many Animals Eat Them." *National Geographic*, January 18, 2019. https://www.nationalgeographic .com/animals/2019/01/many-ocean-creatures-surprisingly-eat-jellyfish/.

Lenz, Petra. "Impact of Environmental Change on Zooplankton Physiology and Reproduction in the Gulf of Alaska." *Research Features,* October 20, 2017. https://researchfeatures.com/2017/10/20/impact-environmental-change-zooplankton-physiology-reproduction/.

Meissner, K. J., A. Montenegro, and C. Avis. "Paleoceanography." In *Encyclopedia of Paleoclimatology and Ancient Environments.* V. Gornitz, ed. New York: Springer, 2008. http://web.science.unsw.edu.au/~katrinmeissner/pdfs/Encyclopedia_meissner.pdf.

"The Microscopic World of Coral." YouTube video, 8:35. Posted by UnderH2OShow, July 16, 2013. https://www.youtube.com/watch?v=CSCUKSVBhSo.

Milstein, Michael. "Saildrones Join NOAA's West Coast Fleet for Experimental Fisheries Surveys." Northwest Fisheries Science Center, NOAA Fisheries, June 2018. https://www.nwfsc.noaa.gov/news/features/saildrone/index.cfm.

"MOCNESS: Multiple Opening/Closing Net and Environmental Sensing System." Woods Hole Oceanographic Institution. Accessed March 2, 2019. http://www.whoi.edu/page.do?pid=8415&tid=7342&cid=10008.

"NOAA's Adopt a Drifter Program." NOAA. Accessed February 4, 2019. https://www.adp.noaa.gov/.

"Norway Lobsters' Appetite for Jellyfish Caught on Camera." Phys.org, January 4, 2018. https://phys.org/news/2018-01-norway-lobsters-appetite-jellyfish-caught.html.

"Ocean Flux Program." Marine Biological Laboratory, University of Chicago. Accessed February 22, 2019. https://www.mbl.edu/ecosystems/conte/ofp/.

Oregon Public Broadcasting. "Drones in Research." Oregon Field Guide. Produced by Ed Jahn, February 2018. https://www.opb.org/television/programs/ofg/segment/drones-research-oregon-state-university/.

Pershing, Andrew J., Line B. Christensen, Nicholas R. Record, Graham D. Sherwood, and Peter B. Stetson. "The Impact of Whaling on the Ocean Carbon Cycle: Why Bigger Was Better." *Plos One,* August 26, 2010. https://journals.plos.org/plosone/article?id=10.1371/journal.pone.0012444.

Profita, Cassandra. "West Coast Fishery Rebounds after Years of Conservation Efforts." OPB, December 13, 2018. https://www.opb.org/news/article/groundfish-recovery-west-coast/.

Riebeek, Holli. "The Gravity of Water." Earth Observatory, NASA, September 12, 2012. https://Earthobservatory.nasa.gov/features/GRACEGroundwater/page1.php.

"Seafloor Mapping AUV." Monterey Bay Aquarium Research Institute. Accessed February 7, 2019. https://www.mbari.org/at-sea/vehicles/autonomous-underwater-vehicles/seafloor-mapping-auv/.

"Sharks: Meet the Seagrass Protectors." National Science Foundation, July 26, 2017. https://www.nsf.gov/discoveries/disc_summ.jsp?cntn_id=242613.

Shearman, Kipp. "How to Use Autonomous Underwater Vehicle Gliders to Make Your Oceanography Better." PowerPoint slides, College of Oceanic and Atmospheric Sciences, Oregon State University. Accessed January 16, 2019. https://www.irso .info/wp-content/uploads/INM2014_Unmanned_Shearman_Kipp.pdf.

Sheppard, Charles. *Coral Reefs: A Very Short Introduction*. Oxford: Oxford University Press, 2014.

Srokosz, M. A., and H. L. Bruden. "Observing the Atlantic Meridional Overturning Circulation Yields a Decade of Inevitable Surprises." *Science* 348, no. 6241. June 19, 2015. https://science.sciencemag.org/content/348/6241/1255575.

The State of World Fisheries and Aquaculture. Food and Agriculture Organization of the United Nations. Rome: FAOUN, Accessed February 18, 2019. http://www.fao .org/3/i9540en/I9540EN.pdf.

"Underwater Frontiers: A Brief History of Seafloor Mapping." NOAA. Accessed February 7, 2019. https://www.arcgis.com/apps/MapJournal/index.html?appid =4718c81ade5e4fada01797fc175c796e.

"What Is a SnotBot?" Ocean Alliance. Accessed February 20, 2019. https://shop .whale.org/pages/snotbot/.

FURTHER INFORMATION

Books

Burns, Loree Griffin. *Tracking Trash: Flotsam, Jetsam, and the Science of Ocean Motion.* Boston: Houghton Mifflin, 2007.
The rogue bath toys and Curtis Ebbesmeyer's work make an appearance in this fascinating *Scientists in the Field* title.

Sardet, Christian. *Plankton: Wonders of the Drifting World.* Chicago: University of Chicago Press, 2015.
This book celebrates the stunning variety of life found under the label "plankton," from miniscule bacteria and viruses to armored diatoms, and from tiny larval fish and crustaceans to siphonophores, the longest organisms in the sea.

Websites

Argo
http://www.argo.ucsd.edu/
Scroll down for more information, including a map that shows the entire Argo fleet.

"Core Questions": NASA
https://climate.nasa.gov/news/2616/core-questions-an-introduction-to-ice-cores/
Read more about ice cores and how they help us learn about past climates.

DEEPEND Consortium: NOVA Southeastern University
http://deependconsortium.org/index.php/gallery/
Look through these amazing photos of the beautiful and bizarre deep-ocean creatures.

GEBCO Seabed 2030 Project: Nippon Foundation
https://seabed2030.gebco.net
Keep tabs on this ambitious effort to map the entire seafloor in high resolution by 2030.

"New DNA Tool 'Changes Everything in Marine Science'": National Geographic
https://www.nationalgeographic.com/environment/2018/12/edna-environmental-dna-counts-fish-changes-marine-science/
Be sure to read through to the end where the article talks about students using eDNA in citizen science projects. So cool!

Ocean Acidification: NOAA
https://www.noaa.gov/education/resource-collections/ocean-coasts-education-resources/ocean-acidification/
Read about the chemical process of ocean acidification, more on why it's so damaging to marine life, and the long-term implications if conditions continue to worsen.

"Ocean Currents: Motion in the Ocean": Smithsonian
https://ocean.si.edu/planet-ocean/tides-currents/ocean-currents-motion-ocean/
Seeing currents in motion makes them easier to understand. This video from
NOAA and the Smithsonian describes three types of currents on our planet and
how they move water around the globe.

Tara Expeditions
https://oceans.taraexpeditions.org/en/
This organization was created and sponsored the Tara Oceans expedition
featured in chapter 5. The website links to all kinds of interesting and
informative ocean resources, and you can also follow current and past
expeditions.

"Vertical Migration: The Largest Movement of Animals on Earth!": Oceanscape
Network and DEEPEND Consortium
http://s3.amazonaws.com/oceanscape-production/file_assets/
files/000/000/196/original/DEEPEND_vertical_migration_poster_
layout_2016_11X17-4.pdf?1465396699
This visual created by the DEEPEND Consortium of scientists offers a concise
look at how vertical migration works.

Windy.com
https://www.windy.com
This fascinating website shows wind patterns around the globe in real time. If
you click on "more layers" and scroll down, you can select "currents." Move the
map to see surface current patterns around the world, including the Gulf Stream
in the Atlantic. You can also select other layers for sea temperatures, swells,
waves, CO2 levels, and more.

Videos

Blue Planet II. London, UK: BBC Studios, 2018.
This video series is a stunning journey through a range of ocean habitats. Look
for it on streaming services or through your local public television station.

Chasing Coral. Directed by Jeff Orlowski.
Produced by Larissa Rhodes. Los Angeles, CA: Exposure Labs, 2017. https://
www.chasingcoral.com. This film from Netflix explores the beauty and plight of
coral reefs around the world, as well as efforts to save them.

"Decoding the Weather Machine." *NOVA, PBS, WGBH Boston*. Aired April 18, 2018.
https://www.pbs.org/wgbh/nova/video/decoding-the-weather-machine/.
This *NOVA* program from 2018 unpacks the science of climate change and how
different aspects of our planet, including the ocean, interact to create climate.

"Earth from Space." *NOVA*, PBS, 56:30. First aired February 13, 2013. https://www
.pbs.org/video/nova-Earth-space/.
See an upwelling lead to a phytoplankton bloom and the feeding frenzy that
follows.

"15 Years of GRACE Earth Observations." YouTube video, 2:30. Posted by NASA, March 15, 2017. https://www.youtube.com/watch?v=fKVPFyu_tHQ. This video from NASA covers what scientists have learned from GRACE about terrestrial water as well as ice sheet loss and sea level rise.

"The Giant Larvacean Bathochordeaus." YouTube video, 4:03. Posted by Monterey Bay Aquarium Research Institute, April 28, 2017. https://www.youtube.com/watch?v=L1wFb_ShW7k. Look at a fascinating sea creature whose discarded "houses" support many ocean detritivores (animals that eat waste).

"Hypoxia: Dead Zone." YouTube video, 4:34. Posted by Karen Meyer, December 2, 2009. https://www.youtube.com/watch?v=yh5Ev8VEbZ0. Researchers Francis Chan and Jack Barth explain why and how hypoxia occurs off the West Coast of the United States.

"Jelly Cam": Monterey Bay Aquarium. https://www.montereybayaquarium.org/animals-and-exhibits/live-web-cams/jelly-cam/. Spend a little time mesmerized by the sea nettles at Monterey Bay Aquarium, and then explore all the ocean-related resources the aquarium has to offer.

"Making Drifter Buoys and Tracking Ocean Currents with NOAA Satellites (Even during a Hurricane)." YouTube video, 12:14. Posted by "TheScienceOf . . . , April 7, 2018." https://www.youtube.com/watch?v=VRuPeDhpMMY. A project in South Florida teaches high school and college students to build their own drifter that uploads data to NOAA satellites and adds to the global understanding of another kind of current—a coastal counter current.

"2012 Visualization Challenge: Observing the Coral Symbiome Using Laser Scanning Confocal Microscopy." YouTube video, 6:14. Posted by Science Magazine, February 8, 2013. https://www.youtube.com/watch?v=al7SIGBVgWo. This video, narrated by Ruth Gates, offers a peek into the lives of coral as seen through a laser scanning confocal microscope.

"What the Vampire Squid Really Eats." YouTube video, 4:32. Posted by Monterey Bay Aquarium Research Institute, September 26, 2012. https://www.youtube.com/watch?v=X8oWnbcLl40. The mysterious vampire squid gives up some of its secrets.

INDEX

ABOUT THE AUTHOR

Christy Peterson's work primarily focuses on science and technology. She especially enjoys illuminating the wonders of nature for her readers, including all things obscure and underappreciated. Recent work includes *Earth Day and the Environmental Movement: Standing Up for Earth, Cutting-Edge Hubble Telescope Data, Breakthroughs in Stars Research, Cutting-Edge Augmented Reality,* and *Cutting-Edge Virtual Reality.* She has written leveled readers covering a variety of topics, from mud buildings to slime. Her work has also been featured in *ASK Magazine* and at the Oregon Museum of Science and Industry.

PHOTO ACKNOWLEDGMENTS

Image credits: ullstein bild/Getty Images, p. 7; NOAA p. 9; Courtesy of Subject, p. 14; Turnervisual/iStock/Getty Images, pp. 16–17; Jay_Zynism/Getty Images, p. 18; Whitney Shefte/The Washington Post/Getty Images, p. 20; Laura Westlund/ Independent Picture Service, pp. 21, 32, 39, 47, 61, 103, 108; NASA, p. 25; StockStudio/Shutterstock.com, p. 31; © Dave Caress/MBARI, p. 33; © Mónika Naranjo González, p. 34; Mlenny/Getty Images, p. 40; © Eleanor Frajka-Williams, p. 42; Gregory Rec/Portland Press Herald/Getty Images, p. 48; Sawaya Photography/ DigitalVision/Getty Images, p. 52; William Luedtke/EyeEm/Getty Images, pp. 54–55; Stocktrek Images/Getty Images, p. 57; Elif Bayraktar/Getty Images, p. 59 (left); De Agostini/Getty Images, p. 59 (right); Sarah Fretwell/Tara Expedition, pp. 64, 65; gorsh13/Getty Images, p. 68; Vittoria Roncalli/University of Barcelona, pp. 71, 74; buccaneership/Getty Images, p. 73; JaysonPhotography/Getty Images, p. 77; Maerie/ Getty Images, p. 78; Placebo365/Getty Images, p. 81; Sergei Krasnoukhov/TASS/ Getty Images, p. 86; atese/Getty Images, p. 87; Wolfgang Kaehler/LightRocket/ Getty Images, p. 88; NOAA/NMFS/NWFSC, p. 92; Ruben Earth/Moment/Getty Images, p. 96; Rapisan Sawangphon/EyeEm//Getty Images, p. 100; Courtesy of Tracey T. Sutton, Ph.D., pp. 106, 110; Courtesy of Nina Pruzinsky, pp. 107, 109; by wildestanimal/Moment/Getty Images, p. 114; Courtesy of Dr. Leigh Torres, p. 118; Posnov/Moment/Getty Images, p. 119; Courtesy of JC Weber/The Ecosystems Center, Marine Biological Laboratory, pp. 123, 125, 126, 127, 128. Background design elements: Jay_Zynism/Getty Images; yoh4nn/iStock/Getty Images; Tendo23/ iStock/Getty Images.

Cover: PixOne/Shutterstock.com; EMstudio- Bonheurem/Shutterstock.com; Jay_ Zynism/Getty Images.